The Carnegie Mellon Anthology of Poetry

The
Carnegie Mellon
Anthology of Poetry

Edited by
Gerald Costanzo and Jim Daniels

Associate Editor, Kathleen Samudovsky

Carnegie Mellon University Press
Pittsburgh 1993

The publication of this book is supported by a grant from the
Pennsylvania Council on the Arts.

Library of Congress Catalog Card Number 92-74533.
ISBN 0-88748-162-0
ISBN 0-88748-163-9 Pbk.
Copyright © 1993 by Gerald Costanzo and Jim Daniels
All rights reserved
Printed and bound in the United States of America

10 9 8 7 6 5 4 3 2 1

This anthology is also published as double issue number 39/40 (the
final issue) of *Three Rivers Poetry Journal*.

Contents

Foreword

We tried to think of a catchy title for this volume. Something which would reflect our continuing enthusiasm for a program, now in its twentieth year, devoted to publishing the work of poets. Ultimately, it seemed most fitting just to call it what it is: *The Carnegie Mellon Anthology of Poetry*. It's a collection by which we celebrate the publication of one hundred titles in the Carnegie Mellon Poetry Series over the past eighteen years; the publication, beginning as the 1980s drew to a close, of seventeen titles of Carnegie Mellon Classic Contemporaries; and it is published as Number 39/40, the final issue, of *Three Rivers Poetry Journal*: a retrospective of the literary magazine inaugurated here in 1973.

The selecting and combining of poems from these three publishing endeavors has been no less formidable—and no less satisfying—a process than was that of the editing and initial publication of the poems. Three Rivers Press, the first stage in the evolution of Carnegie Mellon University Press, was established in 1972. Three Rivers began by publishing a chapbook series: titles by Richard R. O'Keefe, Ann Hayes and Anita Brostoff (on the sonnets of Gladys Schmitt) were followed by early work of Greg Kuzma, Albert Drake, William L. Fox, and Mark Jarman. Though the Carnegie Mellon Poetry Series debuted in 1975 with books by T. Alan Broughton and Ann Hayes, Three Rivers continued to publish under its own imprint until 1979. 1976 saw the first Three Rivers full-length collections, *The Lady From the Dark Green Hills* by Jim Hall and *Petroglyphs* by Sam Hamill, succeeded a year later by John Calvin Rezmerski's *An American Gallery*. Three "new format" chapbooks by Patricia Henley, Richard Hazley, and Richard Harteis rounded out the final year of Three Rivers Press offerings.

Three Rivers Poetry Journal had its inception in a prospectus written by novelist Gladys Schmitt for the founding of the creative writing "option" for undergraduates in the English department. This program was formulated in 1967 and implemented the following year. The journal's first issue, produced shortly after Ms. Schmitt's death in the fall of 1972, was dedicated to her memory. It contained poems by Linda Pastan, Stephen Dunn, William Stafford, Paula Rankin, and Philip Dacey among others. Over the years the journal has published, in chapbook form, the work of a number of poets including Gene Frumkin and Karen Zealand. For a time, beginning with Issue 9 in 1977, *Three Rivers* featured selections of poems by individual poets which were accompanied by commentary on their work. These included Dave Smith (essay by John Gardner), Peter Cooley (Philip Dacey), Patricia Goedicke (Ron Slate), Mary Oliver (Robert Wallace), Brendan Galvin (George Garrett), and Wayne Dodd (Michael Waters and Hilary Masters).

Other "special" issues included Number 6 which was edited and produced entirely by the undergraduates in the advanced poetry workshop in 1975 (among the members were such future poets as Nancy James, Paul Barry, and Lisa Zeidner who—in addition to two collections of poems—has also published three novels); Issue 13/14 was largely given over to reviews of contemporary poetry; 17/18 was our "nomination issue" for which we wrote to a number of widely published poets soliciting their work and asking them to select the work of newer, often unpublished, poets for inclusion; in 27/28 we published our first short fiction and featured stories by Hilary Masters, Kent Anderson, and Stephen Dunn; and 33/34 was a concerted effort to publish only writers who had not previously appeared in the journal. *Three Rivers: Ten Years*, with an introduction by Gerald Stern, (an anthology reviewing the Journal's first decade) was published in 1983. As that volume is still available, our decision (with some exceptions) has been not to reprint poems from its pages here.

The Carnegie Mellon Poetry Series has published an average of six titles annually. Its authors and their collections have received numerous awards ranging from National Endowment for the Arts Fellowships and Guggenheim Fellowships to a citation from the Great Lakes Colleges Association, and have included honors from the Whiting Foundation, the American Academy and Institute of Arts and Letters, grants from various state arts agencies and, of course, the Pulitzer Prize for Poetry which was awarded to Rita Dove for *Thomas and Beulah*. The Classic Contemporaries, a series which reprints titles by important poets, now mostly in their forties and fifties, grew out of conversations—at readings or speaking at writers' conferences around the country—with writers and students who lamented the lack of availability of certain books or that their interest in poetry had arisen long after notable books were out of print.

We feel more than a little remorse that *Three Rivers Poetry Journal* concludes publication with this volume. Certainly twenty years constitute a lengthy life for any little magazine, and perhaps the greater contrition is due the literary periodical which continues only to outlive its own vitality. As for the future, we will continue to publish as much poetry as funding allows, and to pursue our goal (fostered by *Three Rivers Poetry Journal*) of attempting to discover new writers through publishing at least two books each year by poets who have not previously been published by this press.

Gerald Costanzo
Harwich, Massachusetts
September, 1992

Introduction

When I first arrived at Carnegie Mellon University in Fall, 1981, Carnegie Mellon University Press had published 22 books of poetry. Now, twelve years later, the Press is publishing its one hundredth title. In the world of poetry publishing, where presses often fizzle out quickly due to declining energy and resources, that is quite an accomplishment. It has been exciting to witness the growth of the Press into a major force in contemporary poetry; the awards and honors Press poets have received speak for themselves. Gerald Costanzo founded the Press and has been its sole director. For most of that time, he did it while teaching a full load in the English department, with only the help of a handful of student interns.

After Rita Dove won the Pulitzer Prize for Poetry for her book, *Thomas and Beulah*, the university was flooded with phone calls from the media. Jerry was away from Pittsburgh at that time, so I helped the secretary in the English department field some of these calls. After I told the callers that Jerry was out of town, they asked, "Well, isn't there someone else at the Press I can talk to?" All I could say was, "Jerry *is* the Press." Today, Carnegie Mellon University Press is still Gerald Costanzo. If you're ever on campus and ask for the Press's offices, someone will probably simply point down the hall and say, "Jerry's office is down there."

I am pleased to be part of this recognition and celebration of the best Carnegie Mellon University Press and *Three Rivers Poetry Journal* have offered over the years. Unlike many other presses which use judges to select at least a portion of the books they publish, Carnegie Mellon's books have been selected by one editor. As a result, after having read the bulk of what has been published, I expected to be able to characterize what a "typical" CMU/*Three Rivers* poem might be, but the diversity of voices running through these pages made that impossible. One thing all of these poems do have in common is an attention to the craft of poetry. Even while rejecting poems in order to narrow the anthology down to manageable size, I had to respect the effort, the care and attention these poets gave to every single poem. While it was difficult sorting through the thousands of poems—poems which had already made it through a rigorous selection process in order to be published in the first place—it was exciting, challenging work. I hope the poems we've chosen for this anthology in turn excite and challenge you, its readers.

Jim Daniels
Bay Harbor, Florida
October, 1992

Acknowledgments

There are numerous individuals without whose aid and advice the publishing of poetry at Carnegie Mellon University Press could not have been sustained, and I wish to acknowledge them here:

Thanks to my co-editor, Jim Daniels, and our associate editor, Kathy Samudovsky, for their tireless efforts in editing and producing this volume;

to Paul Zimmer for his guidance and generosity, especially in those days when he was assistant director of the University of Pittsburgh Press and editor of the Pitt Poetry Series while I served as a reader for the United States Award contest of the International Poetry Forum;

to Margot Barbour, production manager of the University of Pittsburgh Press, whose technical expertise I have been recipient of on several occasions;

to Alice Halliday for her support at a crucial period in the life of *Three Rivers Poetry Journal*;

to administrators at arts agencies without whose support our program could not have existed: especially Leonard Randolph, literature program director at the National Endowment for the Arts in the mid-1970s, and Peter Carnahan, director of literature programs at the Pennsylvania Council on the Arts, and his successor Marcia Salvatore;

to presidents, provosts, and deans—past and present—at Carnegie Mellon University who have been instrumental in sustaining the Press: Richard Cyert, Robert Mehrabian, Erwin Steinberg, John P. Crecine, Stephen Fienberg, and Peter Stearns;

to the students in my "Editing and Publishing" classes— too numerous to name here, but spanning a twenty year period from Rubin Pfeffer (for many years a designer with Harcourt Brace) to Jack Silbert (now with Scholastic Magazines), and Tracy Perneta (current editorial assistant with the Press), my enduring appreciation of their first professional efforts;

and finally, to my wife, Carla, for her assistance with cover designs: when the attractiveness of our covers has been moderate, the selections and decisions have been mine; for those handsome, sophisticated, and radiant, credit is due her.

G.C.

The Carnegie Mellon Anthology of Poetry

Night: *Volcano, California*

I have been walking for hours on a street called Consolation,
near Jerome, Emigrant, National,
past lit houses with orchards and hoses, where meals are being
                    laid,
and in the yellow squares the figures waver,
while out here, I realize, once again, I am alone.
Tonight I don't mind so much. A porchlight cuts into the
                    darkness like steam,
and falls oddly on an aluminum shed, a red roof suddenly pale,
a toolbox, a child's bicycle.
I think of my friends, lifting me across the years,
while the Plough and the Archer follow each other
at exactly the same distance every night,
and the Swan floats and points its long neck,
and the Oaks drowse, Valleys and Blues.

All day I have been reading
about the invisible world, the one
that's always trying to reach us. What if we could hear
the small round 'o's of dirt,
the chant of stars and plants,
carbon and sulphur, calling to each other, innumerable
to innumerable, a throat at every blade of grass.

A dog walks up Emigrant,
smelling his way home, sniffs me, barks,
And it seems to me now that the night is a sea, is a mouth,
full of fish, full of trees, viburnum smelling like turpentine,
sweetgums thrashing into the wind with their cargo of pods
                    and stars,
and I don't miss the day, though the pole I'm holding in my
                    hand

has turned cold and black as a fossil, and the road seems packed
with bones.

And now something rises, something has been released,
has been waiting, wants to breathe,
there is no stopping it, it rinses the streets of Volcano,
past the rock shop where geodes cool, and feldspar, and mica,
fills the cuff of a trouser leg, and a trench, and a silo,
out to the field where crickets clack their legs in the warm
damp hay
and the stubs of sneezeweed and silverweed
call to the sky, or so I think.

A man coughs. An engine sputters and dies down. I turn down
Emigrant,
I can hardly see Jerome. Night scours the road of detail,
of ordinary gravel, and cancels everything but form.

So that the souls of trees are unlocked. And they pour.

DIANE AVERILL

Bad for You

You think I am
some strange pesticide
sleeping against your skin.
You think a woman
offering herself
is a poisoned apple.

You want me
to make you decaf
espresso. You ask for
popcorn, no
butter, no sex.

You think I want
to crouch like this
along your perfect
silk arteries of
fear all night?
You think I want to be
a gargoyle of your heart?

Renewal

for Joel

In the light falling from old growth trees
I saw Salamander, a burning ember
and here with you at Oceanside Cafe
this is like the swirls of red in your dark beard.
The sun has walked on your skin, set fire to it.
I ask about red-headed relatives.
When you say Grandfather
I see all the way back
before he surfaces in your eyes.

Salamander swam in the creek
but on land he was a slow
flow over red bark
turning back
to earth. He moved aside
to let me pass on the trail
but I sat down with him
the way I sit with you now
in this cafe. Love is war, you say.
No? What is it then?

Salamanders mate slowly, under water.
But you never took your
shoes off on the sand.

I sat with Salamander on
red logs, thoughts breaking down

into earth and we
looked at each other
out of different eyes, curious
and trusting. You and Renardo talk
about women, Ann and I about men,
and though you and I also talk of men and women
we can't convey the differences in talk.

But there is a harmony here,
and grace, the swimming of our thoughts together
that of lizards with soft skins,
where love renews itself
in light growing
tips, and it is different
colors further back.
Love is more than war.
It sets fire to our skin,
brings hidden selves to surface.

MARVIN BELL

Stars Which See, Stars Which Do Not See

They sat by the water. The fine women
had large breasts, tightly checked.
At each point, at every moment,
they seemed happy by the water.
The women wore hats like umbrellas
or carried umbrellas shaped like hats.
The men wore no hats and the water,
which wore no hats, had that well-known
mirror finish which tempts sailors.
Although the men and women seemed at rest
they were looking toward the river
and some way out into it but not beyond.
The scene was one of hearts and flowers

though this may be unfair. Nevertheless,
it was probable that the Seine had hurt them,
that they were "taken back" by its beauty
to where a slight breeze broke the mirror
and then its promise, but never the water.

The Mystery of Emily Dickinson

Sometimes the weather goes on for days
but you were different. You were divine.
While the others wrote more and longer,
you wrote much more and much shorter.
I held your white dress once: 12 buttons.
In the cupola, the wasps struck glass
as hard to escape as you hit your sound
again and again asking Welcome. No one.

Except for you, it were a trifle:
This morning, not much after dawn,
in level country, not New England's,
through leftovers of summer rain I
went out rag-tag to the curb, only
a sleepy householder at his routine
bending to trash, when a young girl
in a white dress your size passed,

so softly!, carrying her shoes. It must be
she surprised me—her barefoot quick-step
and the earliness of the hour, your dress—
or surely I'd have spoken of it sooner.
I should have called to her, but a neighbor
wore that look you see against happiness.
I won't say anything would have happened
unless there was time, and eternity's plenty.

Gemwood

to Nathan and Jason, our sons

In the *shoppes*
they're showing "gemwood":
the buffed-up flakes of dye-fed pines—
bright concentrics or bull's-eyes,
wide-eyed on the rack of
this newest "joint effort
of man and nature." But then

those life-lines circling
each target chip of "gemwood"
look less like eyes, yours or mine,
when we have watched a while.
They are more like the whorls
at the tips of our fingers,
which no one can copy. Even on

the photocopy Jason made of
his upraised hands, palms down
to the machine, they do not appear.
His hands at five-years-old—
why did we want to copy them, and
why does the grey yet clear print
make me sad? That summer,

the Mad River followed us
through Vermont— a lusher state than
our own. A thunderous matinee
of late snows, and then the peak
at Camel's Hump was bleached.
As a yellow pear is to the sky—
that was our feeling. We had with us

a rat from the lab— no, a pet
we'd named, a pure friend who changed
our minds. When it rained near
the whole of the summer, in that

8

cabin Nathan made her a social creature.
She was all our diversion, and brave.
That's why, when she died

in the heat of our car
one accidental day we didn't intend,
it hurt her master first and most,
being his first loss like that,
and the rest of our family felt badly
even to tears, for a heart that small.
We buried her by the road

in the Adirondack Mountains,
and kept our way to Iowa.
Now it seems to me the heart
must enlarge to hold the losses
we have ahead of us. I hold to
a certain sadness the way others
search for joy, though I like joy.

Home, sunlight cleared the air
and all the green's of consequence. Still
when it ends, we won't remember
that it ended. If parents must receive
the sobbing, that is nothing
when put next to the last crucial fact
of who is doing the crying.

JAMES BERTOLINO

The Coons

A four-year-old girl
drowned today in the pond.
Her mother fell on the bank
pounding the greasy water with

her fists. The mud specks
made her tears run brown
off her chin when two old men &
the paperboy took her home
to the trailer. You watched

from our window. When I came back
from the liquor store you said
we can't drink gin tonight.
I told you how coming round a curve
suddenly a raccoon mother & five
little ones, I locked the brakes & slid
watching as, one by one, quickening
their pace just slightly they
came into view to the right of the fender

up the ditch a few feet & turned
to sit in a row, all six of them
smiling.

On a Line by John Ashbery

The space was
magnificent & dry.
You slid your

cold hands up
beneath my sweater
whispering "I love

your body" to my ear
that I not be surprised
by the chill. Your chin

resting on my shoulder.
Together we watched
a lone gull bring down

the sun. An abrupt
shrill cry. Somewhere
off along the beach

the small life
of a bird or chipmunk
was complete.

The Landscape

I draw a line from
edge to edge
to provide place, a land-

scape within which
to begin. Birds

float down from a great height
across the page, wings
like paper kites

brushing air, eyes
flashing the
landing lights

of the 747
gear unfolding seat-
belt warning holds

our attention the squeak
stomachs clutching
as cement grabs rubber

you touch my hand it's
been nice Jim maybe we'll run

into each other someplace honey.

Michael Blumenthal

Blue

"the blue that will always be there as it is now..."
— Georgia O'Keefe, on her painting, *"Pelvis III"*

Inside the hollowness that is bone
and the hollowness that is us, blue
is how it has always been and how
it will always be: the blue acres
of flesh we have traveled in search
of the propinquitous night, the blue
hours of morning before the mist rises
over the lake, the blue gaze of the sycamore
over empty fields in February. Now,
it is dark and my bones open over the blue
sheets of the bed to welcome the night.
I gaze into the pale blue of your eyes
and see that I, too, am turning blue
like the graceful dead in their blue parlors
of silk and sweet dreaming. Last night,
the swallows prancing over the fields
were blue, and in the star-swift glide
of sky over the clouds, I realized
we end as we began, and moved along:
blue baby, blue sky, sweet blue grief,
the deep blue of no more breathing.
Tempera on paper or oil on canvas,
it is the blue envelope of the voice
that says *I love you*, and when the bones
open out into their pelvic dust, the blue
that is always blue is always there.

Juliek's Violin

"Was it not dangerous, to allow your vigilance to fail, even for a moment, when at any minute death could pounce upon you? I was thinking of this when I heard the sound of a violin, in this dark shed, where the dead were heaped on the living. What madman could be playing the violin here, at the brink of his own grave? It must have been Juliek ... The whole of his life was gliding on the strings— his lost hopes, his charred past, his extinguished future. He played as he would never play again."

— Elie Wiesel, Night

"Alnest Du den Schopfer, Welt?" ("World, do you feel the Maker near?")

— Schiller, Ode to Joy

In the dank halls of Buchenwald,
a man is playing his life.

It is only a fragment from Beethoven—
soft, melodic, ephemeral as the sleep
of butterflies, or the nightmares of an infant,
but tonight it is his life.

In one hand, he holds the instrument,
resonant with potential. In the other,
the fate of the instrument: hairs
of a young horse strung between wood,
as the skin of a lampshade is strung between wood.

The bow glides over the strings, at first,
with the grace of a young girl brushing her hair.
Then, suddenly, Juliek leans forward
on his low stool. His knees begin to quiver,
and the damp chamber fills with a voice
like the voice of a nightingale.

Outside, the last sliver of light
weaves through the fence. A blackbird
preens its feathers on the lawn as if

to the music, and a young child watches
from the yard, naked and questioning.

But, like Schiller crying out—
Ahnest Du den Schopfer, Welt—
Juliek plays on.

And the children,
as if in answer,
burn.

ANNE C. BROMLEY

Slow Men Working in Trees

You saw a sign once: SLOW— MEN WORKING IN TREES
and you thought it was perfect
for slow men to be working in trees, that a tree
is the only place where a slow man can work
without fear of being rushed
into completing what a quick man puts before him.

You are an engineer and measure the slowness
of men working against your highways, your bridges.
They never see the heart
of your plans. They hesitate and you want to break
their slanted drawing boards.

It comes as no surprise to you that they have left
the drawing room for trees, that they work slowly
into the night while you try to sleep
next to a woman with no patience for slow men.
Drawing the curtain doesn't help. You hear the branches
tapping on the pane.

They must know that this is the hour least easy to bear
as you ask what right
slow men have to be working in your tree.
You decide it must come down and repeat this aloud
to the woman next to you. You hear yourself screaming
above the scratches on the window
that tomorrow the slow men will be gone
and you will be left alone with their sign.

My Mother's Face Never Moved

throughout the funeral . . . even as her nails
dug into my skin when the elegy was said
she wore no black
or gray . . . reminding me that Lou Burgess hated
black on women
unless the neckline plunged or the back was open
my mother wore green, pine green
and her hair was coiffed in a way I remember
a long time ago in a photograph
with Lou
with my father
with Lou's wife . . .
Lou's son and I were playing with trains
in the basement . . . a party upstairs
the tinkle of glass, Lou's deep laugh
my mother winking at him from across the room
I went up for Cokes
and saw Lou's hand on my mother's waist
in the crowded kitchen . . . he filled the empty glasses
then sent me off
back down to the basement
I got tired of watching those wormy trains
the planned breakdowns
the fake collisions
the rubber tunnel in the rubber mountain
and the stupid toy soldiers trying to sabotage

the same old tracks . . . I kept listening
for whole sentences upstairs, some clue
to the dirty words that fell like tinsel
on a naked pine

Teel St. Trailer Court

Marigolds in a white box. No love
has yet been made. Only white cattle
floating through the tall grass.
Their eyes, heavily lidded, blink at the sun
melting first light on the soft curve of road.

There are men and women living in trailers.
Their lights are tiny suns rising above checkered curtains.
There is no time for making love.
Their shadows move about the small rooms,
packing bag lunches, drinking instant coffee,
their fingers tapping on formica counters.

He will drop her off at Hubbell Lighting,
driving on to Corning Glassworks.
He will pick her up at four, drive on
to Little People Day Care where
their son has been fingerpainting blue suns and purple grass.

Son and mother mow the lawn. His short legs and toy mower
echo her longer stride.
His tennis shoes dry on the porch. His tee-shirts
blow urgently on the clothesline.

His father puzzles under the hood of a red MG;
he believes there is no reason why
he cannot get it back on the road. Goldenrod
surrounds the cinderblocks, and the lights go out
at ten o'clock. No love has yet been made
as the cornflowers bloom before dawn.

T. ALAN BROUGHTON

Lyric

*"Don't let's forget that the little emotions are the great captains
of our lives, and that we obey them without knowing it,"*
— *Van Gogh, to his brother Theo.*

First flakes of winter seen through glass
of a train that takes me to school.

Wren, confused, who sings at night
in the glade, and I wake glad
to be uncertain where I am.

In another room my father speaks
in low tones not to wake me—
but I am cool, the fever past,
and the voice a caress.

Under the boughs of the copper beech
shade so deep that I only see
the bright lawn I have left.

My child chanting himself to sleep.
I do not turn the page of my book.

Each day ending like this:
my hand in hers as we accept
our time for dreams,
and the Landscape with Bridge
keeps its place all night.

Poplars are bordered blue,
cows graze at ease near a river,
and each second that shimmers
with leaves and invisible stars
is a small poem.

Hold, Hold

We lay still
          our two worlds
laced as hands
when you said *look*
and we watched a mouse begin
a strange descent
along the piping to the lamp.

We could tell by the way
he paused
to close his eyes as if
pain took him in his gut
that he had taken
poison we'd set out.

          Naked
I rose and fetched a pail
a lead pipe
          nudged him into it
started to bear him out
when you said *maybe*
you should drown him.

          It was
kindness to fill the pail with water
watching his fur go sleek
as he tried the slick sides
not a sound as he paddled
all of it held in the black eyes
not even looking at me
          but deeper into
the swirl of all things

and then I held him under
with pipe against the side
his feet jerking
small bubbles and a spot of blood

issuing from his nose
                    and myself held
in the steel sides
our chalice brimming with ripples going out
into shivering grass
the trees bending away
birds suddenly flying back
hawk in a plummet
                    its strings
cut
and all that night the stars
wheeled angrily like motes
in a muddied spring
                    where I am
getting in deeper
in deeper in
deeper.

Serenade for Winds

"We know life so little that it is very little in our power to distinguish right from wrong, just from unjust, and to say that one is unfortunate because one suffers, which has not been proved."

— *Van Gogh, to his brother Theo and sister-in-law Jo.*

Clustered beside the road are a van,
pick-up, two sedans. In another season
we might imagine hunters tracking deer
or lugging sixpacks away from their wives.
But the Seal of State on one door warns
a new fact has burned its brand on the landscape.

From the vacant truck a radio plays
Mozart into the summer breeze.
Now an oboe floats above
the bass of bassoon, a clarinet
lures the horn to join

this conversation on the waves.

We have stopped to check the map
but might believe that only this
was why we drove for hours—
leaves lifted in a freshet,
all else forgotten and offstage
when air and music are one.

In the forest a trooper stops
a witness from cutting the rope
with his knife. Procedures require
cameras and tape, a careful report.
A man's body, halted by noose
and gravity, slowly swings
from the maple's limb.
In an hour or two a wife
and elder son will try
through taut jaw to say
they're not surprised, blame him,
the State, or bank, or all.

Only a few bars remain.
Cut him down. Let him drop
on the layered leaves.
The notes rise into the silence of air
through which the body must descend.

MICHAEL DENNIS BROWNE

Talk to Me, Baby

1

A friend at a cocktail party tells me
of being on a fishing trip up North
and meeting some men from Illinois

who showed him how to clean and filet a fish properly;
and of how, when one particular pike
was stripped almost clean, almost all of him gone,
the jaw with the razory teeth opened
and some kind of cry came from the creature,
that head on the end of almost no body;
and the man with the knife said:
"Talk to me, baby."

2

Up in the Boundary Waters last weekend
I hooked a trout, my first, and played him.
I got him to the shallows
and tried to raise him. And the women
got down into the water with my leather hat—
we hadn't brought a net—and I was yelling
"I've got a fish! I've got a fish!"
out into the evening, and they tried
to get him into the hat, and did once,
but then he was out again—a wriggle, a flap—
that fish jumped out of my hat!—
and the line, gone loose, jerked, snapped, and he was back
in the water, the hook in him.

And he didn't turn into
a glimmering girl, like he did for
young Willie Yeats,
nor was he a Jesus, like for Lawrence;
he just drifted head down near the shallows,
huge, the huge hook in him.
And Louis and Phil came up in the other
canoe, and we got the flashlight on him,
and tried to get hold of him. But then, somehow,
we lost him, drifting about, he was not there
but gone somewhere deeper into the water,
every minute darker; my hook in him.

I hooked five or six snags after that, yelling
each time that each one was a fish, bigger

than the last. But I brought nothing living up.
And the other canoe went ghostly on the water,
silvery, like a dish with two quiet eggs in it;
and the pines were massed, dark, and stood and smelled
strong, like a bodyguard of dried fish.

3

Breathing, my brother in my house,
and breathing, his wife beside him.

Breathing, my brother in America,
his body in my bed, her body.

Their tent the color of the sun in my garden.
And they are riding West.

And both of us riding West, brother,
since we swam out of the father,

heading, six years apart,
the same way.

The dog stares at me, not knowing
why I have not fed him.
The cat crying to come in.

Whom we feed, sustain us.
Who need us, we keep breathing for.

I have seen you, at supper with friends,
put your hands to the guitar strings

and bring strong music out, seen you
sit and pick out

a tune on the piano,
on a friend's penny whistle.

To hold an instrument, to play.
To hold a pen, to write.

To do as little harm as possible
in the universe, to help

all traveling people, West, West;
you are not traveling alone,

not ever; we all go with you;
only the body stays behind.

4

When I stand on my island, a Napoleon,
one hand nailed to my chest,
the writing hand;

when I can only *stare*
at the ocean, at the birds
running and turning against the light . . .

When I am
the Illinois man and his kind,
"Talk to me, baby,"

the one with the knife inside, sometimes,
the one you may meet on your travels,
the one behind you in the line to get on the bus,

the one arranging a deal in a phone booth
as you drive past,
when I become that thing I sometimes become,

I will go into
the green of this visit, the green
you asked me to try to see

after my earlier, darker poems for you—
and this, the fourth one, darker
than I meant, since the man with the knife

swam into it— O when that killer
stands over our city, our sleeping and loving places,
tent, canoe, cabin of sweet people—

I will hear with your ears
the songs of the birds of the new world
that so quicken you, and look for

their wings that flame and flash—there!—
among the leaves and branches . . .

5

Too often I have wanted
to slip away, the hook in me,
to roll off the bed
and into the dark waters under it;
to drift, head down,
hide, hide, the hook in me;
to roll
in the wet ashes of the father,
wet with the death of the father,
and not try
to burn my way upward; the son, rising.

I swear to you now, I will survive,
rise up, and chant my way through these losses;

and you, you, brother, whatever that is,
same blood, you who swim
in the same waters,
you promise me to make *your* music too,
whatever the hurt;

O when we are almost only
mouth, when we are almost only a head
stuck on the pole of the body,
and the man says "Talk to me, baby,"
let's refuse him, brother, both, all of us,
and striking the spine like an instrument, inside,
like birds, with even the body broken
our feathers fiery—there! there!—among
the leaves and branches, make
no sounds he will know;
like birds, my brother, birds of the new world, *sing*.

Epithalamion/Wedding Dawn

for Nicholas & Elena

1

Happy the man who is thirsty.
And the moths, pilgrims to our screens.
The fisher stands waist-deep in the water,
waiting.   Happy the man waiting.

Who is not alone?   Who does not sleep
in the dark house of himself, without music?
The world, a collapsed fire, shows only its smoke,
and the smoke hides its hills,

hides, too, the places where we are sleeping,
the hand opened, the hand closed.
Fragments, the lovers lie.   And the question,
saying:

Who is broken?   No one is broken,
but the living are sleeping, like animals,
like the dead.   Tree dreams
of the man he was, who walked

by the shore, who followed
the hill upward, who dragged his roots
through the universe, who lay down
to suffer there, and, loving the earth,

left it exhausted, returned to it renewed.
But the house is dark.   The sky at such time
has no light.   Even the lines in the hand
are a little desert without name, and silent.

2

Friends; in the hours before dawn; the day of your wedding.
What will I tell you then?
That solitude's thorn
breaks into bloom now?   I think it is so.
I think that if we are scarred, light heals us now.
We can be heard, making our difficult music.
And for this the sun
drags itself up from the dark parts of the world,
again, again.
The windows take on the peculiar fire of the living.
The dog hoots like a wood-pigeon, he has *his* morning.

3

You must not be angry with this planet.
For we are in a company
whose music surpasses its pain.
For I tell you, I sat in the dark, also,
and the wedding light came onto my window,
and the hills were cleared for me,
and the field spread out in front of me, remarkable, like marble.
And I thought: this is their day,
how it breaks for them!
O sir, the angel flies, even with bruises
O lady, a bird can wash himself anywhere.
The dawn that came up the day of your wedding

took me in its hand like the creature I am;
and I heard the dark that I came from
whispering 'Be silent'.
And the dawn said 'Sing'.
And I found the best words I could find around me,
and came to your wedding.

ANN CARREL

Catching

When I was five I didn't know bats.
But one morning my brother's skinny hand
Flicked one loose from under the picnic table
And into a mason jar;
Then the sinewy muscles of my brother's arms,
Which were not quite muscles yet,
Tightened the lid.

The bat looked me square in the face
And screamed for all the world like I should know,
Held me to account though I was five,
Opened up its jaws and clenched
The teeth like diamond pins, over and over,
And all the screaming echoing the fix that it was in.

I suppose you have heard that scream,
The kind catfish make
When they're beached and have a treble hook
Lost deep somewhere,
And the scream is really gill plates rubbing
Muscle and gristle,
But fish are noncommittal and look at the sky
With the one eye, until it films.

The Treacherous Death of Jesse James

"It was little Bobby Ford,
That dirty little coward,
Who laid poor Jesse in his grave."

It would be Eddie
Sitting on the wooden porch
After breakfast, leaning
Against the screen door and
Making it bang with his elbow maybe.
Inside,
Jesse smells that grass
Through dusty screen wires,
The creak of the springs on the wind feels
Sharp on his shoulder blades.
Standing on a chair in the parlor,
His sock feet clinging
Slightly to the crack in the cane seat,
He wipes the haze of dust from across a face,
His face when he was twelve
Or someone's face who was
Or likely was,
Framed in wood with gilded edgings,
Rubbed with his sleeve and bang
As he turns his head,
The gilt edges blending in his hair when he was twelve;
Son not so hard.

KELLY CHERRY

Going Down on America

Turned on to the transcendent, he holds her
in his arms, strokes her sunny hair.
Such sweet skin is coming into view
as the clothes of Straight are shed

over New Jersey & kicked aside
into the wide Missouri River—

He pledges allegiance to lightfilled breasts,
to the drops of shine spilled
on Shenandoah's applerich harvest.

In this union of smoke & suck he enters a state just west
of grace where Wyoming is what cowboys do
on Saturday night when the boss has paid them up
& the wind smells of Montana carried downstream,
clean but unmistakable.

O Mount Rushmore,
move him to your eye of stone!
In wheat fields he may dream
of stalks of sun,

discover blue shadows
in the shingles of the fallen pinecone!

The seventh day dawns somewhere above the fabulous Sierras,
so high he can scarcely see it,
& in a whirlwind of contradiction funnels itself south
into the dusk of his throat,
enlightens his heart,
& sets the flesh to dancing upon bare bones
across known borders
into a land lost
to reality.

GILLIAN CONOLEY

Some Gangster Pain

Eunice is tired of pain, everyone else's.
She wants some gangster pain,

to strut her thick ivories
in a collision of dreams, the pajamas-to-work
dream, the magnolia siege dream.

What ya got there, Eunice, say Johnny and the boys.
Eunice lives behind the bus,
another fleeing place,
riot of exhaust. She doesn't
have much to say,
but she says it, hello.

When the boys talk
she feels her skirt
shift to the corner she took.
She sees them snap their fingers
to no dog. She knows

they wouldn't understand.
She knows her feet point themselves forward
but she keeps walking backwards in rain,
her heels too fast, or the rain seeps
into trees, she can't tell. She likes this street.

Johnny and the boys got on
jackets that twitch.
Eunice wears a lot of accessories. The boys
paint a circle on the wall
the color of lips.

I'd Like a Little Love in the Wine-red Afternoon

I'd like a little love in the wine-red afternoon.
I'm not ashamed to enter naked into anybody's room.
New skin, old vein. Poppies shudder

in the garden over a soldier's stone feet, over ants
trailing back and forth. The gardener is a river god
misting rows of boxwood parched by heat.

By night he carries shadow money
to the empty world of things, in his chic black clothes.
And I throw back my head.

I saw the cord grow taut that binds
our marrow to the earth.
I saw another nothing in the universe.

The gardener walks through beds of iris
like the brief blue lights of matches
in a garden dug with knives

in the wine-red afternoon.
I'm not ashamed to enter naked
into anybody's room.

Unchained Melody

Out of the part of the earth
that arches from the sun, out
of the part that disobeys,
where having no walls to stay them
convict pictures tumble
down post office steps
and the whole town
lies etched in charcoal,
all my larks are ravens,
and the population
numbers a woman who has come
straight out of the earth
knee-deep in gorgeous raw material
with no melody around
to cheat on the words.

She's got a mind to sleep
in the arms of society tonight.
A hill is pliable as a knee.
Cold mountain stream

like a hand mirror to fan the dreamers,
to brush the pollen
from her thighs . . .

Each evening she looks down to see
how we are coming along
with the scaffold.
The shade tree states
rustle beneath the moon, and then
the hay state,
the chainsaw state,
the state of snowy roadsides.

Not a girl of salt
in sight, no unearthed Eurydice
seeking lament, nobody's
underground love. And Phoebe-notes
don't pierce from the trees,
nor the gestures
of a woman jump-cutting
a staircase . . .

The rose in her hand
drooping and gently hurt,
she eats dirt if she has to,
but drinks from her own well.

And now a foxcoat is stretched out in the sunrise.
Breath of wind. Red darkness of dawn,
her great poker face.

PETER COOLEY

Ararat

This is the room where summer ends.
This is the view, a single window

opening to evening: banks of clouds,
shivering to be called down quickly,
step forward, naked, to greet me.

How beautiful each is, assuming
animal form on the lawn
never known before, with beaks & tusks
silver, their feathers, fluttering, gold.
Quivering, they pair off, pair off

till I wonder if the ark has docked tonight
for me. I am not ready yet
though darkness falls from the air
& I have dreamed of this. I've got to pack,
I've got to be wished well by somebody

familiar. The animals are darkening,
calling. They are wading the dark, thrashing.
And now their ivory fetlocks, their horns,
demand an answer going down, *Are you coming*
before the waves close over us, are you.

So. This is my night to leave
carrying nothing, the wind between my eyes,
no one to clear the room of me
or to lie down with me even once.
No one saying the dark is not enough.

The Elect

Many the shadowless under the rose leaves
untrembling midmorning.
Many at early evening
the wings, ochre, henna, cinnabar,
which continue, unseen, singing
when night, never stirring, takes their air.

In this garden out of time
the stillborn until their moment linger.

Their souls climb the white down
of little tubers, footless; they suck
mouthless the orris root. Hoarfrost
their spoor foreshadows them, burned off by noon.

And from this place we called the child to us
that you might carry it
to give it up. And spare her breath
this life, the agony of body, the next, the next, the next.
Tonight on the long, clear wing of her voice
the soul of our daughter walks out
between the thorns, uplifted, no one

warbling her absence, everlasting.

The Loom

Unless light be applied to it like a poultice
sex will not heal in us.
It is a wound less scabrous than any.
Therefore, invisible, Vincent set down here
the landlady's daughter, then the widow, then the whore,
within this little gnome upright over a thread
and composed the man in himself he must have lost
to lust for three women in succession hopelessly.
Or did he sit his ghost inside this frame
and spin out Margot who threatened death after he fled?
Whatever, the facts wash off in this clear air,
reduced to a clean Dutch radiance
which sets all things at such rigid angles to each other
they assume the attitude of prayer.
Kneel down, little weaver, in the falling light,
your heart is a bobbin, it cannot stop
thrashing and trembling even if the shuttle stop.
The loom is a cage. Our bodies are another.
The light falls, a man and woman trade their threads in it.
The light fails and they stumble, fall in it.
They move through each other, they touch and separate.
They find themselves raveled in the expanse of a great cloth.

The Other

When you come to the other side
of lust the body lays itself
down in others as itself
no longer and the fields till now
fallow, bloom, vermillion.

When you cross to the other side
of pride the heart withers
into tinder, the wind blesses it.
Your body flares, white sticks
this side of anger.

Arriving at the other side
of terror the voice is a dark flame
walking evenings in the garden,
your name unknown to it
if the last light calls you.

And when you have passed the other side
of hope the shore will blaze
finally. We are all light here.
Do not look for me or ask.
You will never have known me.

MICHAEL CUDDIHY

Steps

for Andy Meyer

She sees him on her way home from work,
grey-haired, stooping to measure the pavement,
something about his slow shuffle that haunts her.
Scanning the worn cheeks, the vagrant bathrobe and slippers,

she falls in beside him, brown hand gentle at his elbow.
Soon they are climbing the long steps, one after one.
At the door, her grave smile invites him to enter.
She guides the frail body down
the hall to the dining room where he can see beyond,
his face beginning to brighten.
He murmurs something in a strange tongue as he watches the
        sunlight
embossing itself on so many leaves, flowers.
If he were Persian he would recognize the word
Paradise means a walled garden,
as if a door had opened and he was standing there, dazed,
in another life, his mind flooded,
past and future one intricate tapestry:
a walled garden. His halting
words struggle to erase the distances.
She makes out the words "sun and snow" and knows he's there,
Russia, a time vanished. Endless
fields, a haze of golden wheat level with the eye. Harvest:
small knots of men wade in, their scythes
moving in wide powerful arcs. A long pile of fresh-
cut fir stacked against the barn. In the near
distance a river gleams and goes out, gleams again.
The old eyes bless her. "Sun and snow," he repeats,
the one phrase saying itself now.

The Pendulum

It doesn't matter if you are late or early,
whether the person you hope to see will actually be there.
Nor even if you get to see her anytime, ever.
It does not matter that, late, you feel uneasy, missing
your heart's desire— desire the root of our pain
with 'our knowledge of this world, like grief, incomplete.'
All is flux, even the chosen changing, changing: the woman
in the white linen dress, the one
with the grey gulls perched there, riding her hips as she walks,
        shoulders

shifting, walks up the ramp from the arrival gate,
her black bag swinging like a pendulum between sadness and
    happiness,
with its package that must be opened, yes a package,
not to be opened prematurely,
even by the one who leans forward now, hunting
the moment to plant his kiss.

This Body

Each time breath draws through me,
I know it's older than I am.
The haggard pine that watches by the door
Was here even before my older brothers.
It's a feeling I get when I pick up a stone
And look at its mottled skin, the grey
Sleeve of time.
This body that I use,
Rooted here, this spur of hillside, leaves shaking in wind,
Was once as small as a stone
And lived inside a woman.
These words, even—
They've come such a long way to find me.
But the sleep that translates everything
Moves in place, unwearied, the whole weight of the ocean
That left us here, breathless.

PHILIP DACEY

Small Dark Song

The cherry-tree is down, and dead, that was so high,
And Wind, that did this thing, roams careless while you cry,
For Wind's been everywhere today, and has an alibi.

Porno Love

for Darlene and Mae

You send me a photograph
of you in which your genitals
are not only exposed
but offered close-up to the lens
like a piece of good advice.
I've never met you
though you say,
"We think you're swell."
I appreciate the gesture:
I've been exposing my genitals
in poems for a long time now,
at least when they're good.
So I know you mean nothing obscene
by it. Your squat is humble,
as mine is, even now.
I am writing this poem
naked, up close.
I am writing it with my penis.
No one but you two sisters
will understand
how such a poem is innocent,
how, as with a confidence to a friend,
no shock is intended,
how what we stick in the faces of our loved ones
is our way of saying, I trust you will not
seal me shut
or cut me off, I love you that much.
Surely we will meet with our clothes on,
that is the point.
But when I say, Thanks for the picture, Girls,
it's nicely cropped,
and you say, We liked the feel of your poem,
I'll be thinking how certain private parts
made vulnerable
give greatest pleasure
in a consummation
of good will.

Looking at Models in the Sears Catalogue

These are our immortals.
They stand around
and always look happy.
Some must do work,
they are dressed for it,
but stay meticulously
clean. Others
play forever,
at the beach, in backyards,
but never move
strenuously. Here
the light is such
there are no shadows.
If anyone gestures,
it is with an open
hand. And the smiles
that bloom everywhere
are permanent, always
in fashion.
                    So
it is surprising to discover
children here,
who must have sprung
from the dark of some loins.
For the mild bodies
of these men and women
have learned to stay
dry and cool:
even the undressed
in bras and briefs
could be saying,
It was a wonderful dinner,
thank you so much.
                    Yet,
season after season,
we shop here:
in Spring's pages,
no ripe abundance

overwhelms us;
in Winter's pages
nothing is dying.
It is a kind of perfection.
We are not a people
who abide ugliness.
All the folds in the clothing
are neat folds,
nowhere to get lost.

How I Escaped from the Labyrinth

It was easy.
I kept losing my way.

CARL DENNIS

The Miracle

One by one, as is human, we may remember,
Far from our meeting places, in the privacy of our rooms,
A child who needed more time than we budgeted,
A mother or father we didn't honor enough,
A friend we failed to be loyal to.
But as a nation our mind is clear.

One by one we may yield to the frog-voice of remorse,
But as a nation we're tuned to an oracle sweeter
And clearer than any in Rome or Jerusalem, a prophet
With a silky baritone who says we've always sided
With the poor and powerless groaning around the world
Whose hardships are worse than the export duties
Levied from England and a tax on tea.

One by one we may be greedy, careless, and ignorant,
And know it, and pray for the grace to be otherwise.

But as a nation we know humility is an error
Praised as a virtue when the Christians were powerless,
When they envied the great-souled,
Great-mannered, pagan princes who overflowed with life
Like gods and were loved as gods are,
The happy gods that can do no wrong.

Nuts and Raisins

No wars allowed now for the true faith,
The faith that mothered us.
And none for the faith we shaped ourselves
In the light of reason and the march of history.
Only the war to keep all self-annointed
True believers from seizing power.
No one strolling the beach,
Filling his pockets with colored stones,
Is allowed to force the edges together later
At the table in the dining room and claim
They're puzzle pieces in a photograph of the Earth
Taken from a fixed star to make clear
How the planets embody the nine moods of the soul.
No cries of Eureka for us, no triumphant phone calls
To the boardroom at Central Planning.
This morning we wander along the beach for driftwood
Tossed up after the night-long gale.
With a little shaping we can use it as a chair
In the newly-converted fire station or grain mill
That we call our cottage.
Today we improvise the part of the landlord.
Tomorrow we're guests getting used to a guestroom
With a fire pole up the middle,
With a mill wheel for a bedstead.
And then we're hikers pausing to rest.
A note on the table points to the jars
Of nuts and raisins under the floor boards.
A map marks the path to the spring house through the woods.
Once the road by the door pointed in one direction;

Now it branches every which way and winds around.
Every tree is reason enough for a detour.
Every memorial stone where somebody sat and thought
How foolish of him to feel lost
Merely because he wasn't sure who he was
And was on his way to no place in particular.

GREGORY DJANIKIAN

Agami Beach
Alexandria, 1955

There were the black flags flying
All along the beach and we knew
We could not swim. There was the sea
Turning too dark and churlish
And there was someone wading in
Too far and standing for a moment
Half in air, half in water.
There was the sand shifting easily
Under his heels and the current
Sweeping him out and out.
There were the cabanas and the sound
Of my sister crying and my feet
Were burning as I ran toward them
But there was my father moving already
Rope in hand sprinting to the water's
Edge and plunging into the sea.
There was my sister crying
"Don't let him go, don't let him die"
And I grew angry at feeling
Her fear, hearing those words.
There was the long line of watchers
And my father's head weaving
In and out of the waves, his arm
Around the other, a speck of light
In the darkness. There was the fear

I shook off as my father
Shook off the sea emerging,
Dragging the body along the hot white sand.
There was the skin blue like water,
There were fingernails the color of plums.
There was my father standing above it
Spent and awkward and full of mercy.
There were the people running toward it
From all directions and there was someone
Pulling us away and my sister crying
"Take it back, take it back!"
It was getting dark. The sea-birds
Were calling to one another, diving,
And no one was moving.

                              Years later,
My sister would suddenly say:
"The colors were all wrong.
I remember the day by its colors."
We were sitting at a table
All afternoon drinking wine
And calling up one name after another
Of friends we had almost forgotten.
Mourad, Nadia, where were they now?
We had been telling old stories
About ourselves, our lives.
We had been laughing.
I remember the blue tablecloth.
Our empty glasses were filling with sunlight.
There was a bowl full of ripe plums.

When I First Saw Snow
Tarrytown, N.Y.

Bing Crosby was singing "White Christmas"
        on the radio, we were staying at my aunt's house
        waiting for papers, my father was looking for a job.
We had trimmed the tree the night before,
        sap had run on my fingers and for the first time

I was smelling pine wherever I went.
Anais, my cousin, was upstairs in her room
    listening to Danny and the Juniors.
Haigo was playing Monopoly with Lucy, his sister,
    Buzzy, the boy next door, had eyes for her
    and there was a rattle of dice, a shuffling
    of Boardwalk, Park Place, Marvin Gardens.
There were red bows on the Christmas tree.
It had snowed all night.
My boot buckles were clinking like small bells
    as I thumped to the door and out
    onto the grey planks of the porch dusted with snow.
The world was immaculate, new,
    even the trees had changed color,
    and when I touched the snow on the railing
    I didn't know what I had touched, ice or fire.
I heard, "I'm dreaming . . ."
I heard, "At the hop, hop, hop . . . oh, baby."
I heard "B & O" and the train in my imagination
    was whistling through the great plains.
And I was stepping off,
I was falling deeply into America.

How I Learned English

It was in an empty lot
Ringed by elms and fir and honeysuckle.
Bill Corson was pitching in his buckskin jacket,
Chuck Keller, fat even as a boy, was on first,
His t-shirt riding up over his gut,
Ron O'Neill, Jim, Dennis, were talking it up
In the field, a blue sky above them
Tipped with cirrus.
                        And there I was,
Just off the plane and plopped in the middle

Of Williamsport, Pa. and a neighborhood game,
Unnatural and without any moves,
My notions of baseball and America
Growing fuzzier each time I whiffed.

So it was not impossible that I,
Banished to the outfield and daydreaming
Of water, or a hotel in the mountains,
Would suddenly find myself in the path
Of a ball stung by Joe Barone.
I watched it closing in
Clean and untouched, transfixed
By its easy arc before it hit
My forehead with a thud.
                              I fell back,
Dazed, clutching my brow,
Groaning, "Oh my shin, oh my shin,"
And everybody peeled away from me
And dropped from laughter, and there we were,
All of us writhing on the ground for one reason
Or another.
                 Someone said "shin" again,
There was a wild stamping of hands on the ground,
A kicking of feet, and the fit
Of laughter overtook me too,
And that was important, as important
As Joe Barone asking me how I was
Through his tears, picking me up
And dusting me off with hands like swatters,
And though my head felt heavy,
I played on till dusk
Missing flies and pop-ups and grounders
And calling out in desperation things like
"Yours" and "take it," but doing all right,
Tugging at my cap in just the right way,
Crouching low, my feet set,
"Hum baby" sweetly on my lips.

PATRICIA DOBLER

His Depression

He said it was like a black bird
sitting on his chest & if he moved
the bird clawed in, raked flesh.
He knew about birds, their light bones
filled with air, so why this black specific hole
where his heart should be? It wasn't fair.

Sometimes, he said, only one thought gave him pleasure:
his father's shotgun, packed with grease,
that he could wipe & carry to the waiting boat,
the first day of duck season & the first light breaking.

1920 Photo

Here is Grandpa, who did not want America,
flanked by children, wife and brother,
brother's wife and children. . . . Standing
to one side, a Chinese woman.

How did she get into this picture!
The mustachioed men, their women proud
in white lace blouses, a solemn occasion . . .
and the Chinese woman in a stiff bright robe,

her eyes shining into mine. My mother can't,
none of my aunts can tell me; but they
are children here, see their rosy faces.
Except for the Chinese woman, everyone touches

everyone else, all of them are making it
in America, even though Grandpa cries for Hungary

at harvest-time, even if he is a landless farmer
who shovels slag at the rolling mill.

Even the Chinese woman, who no one alive remembers,
who migrated into my family's picture
like a jungle bird among chickens,
looks happier to be here than my Grandpa.

STEPHEN DOBYNS

Black Dog, Red Dog

The boy waits on the top step, his hand on the door
to the screen porch. A green bike lies in the grass,
saddlebags stuffed with folded newspapers. The street
is lined with maples in full green of summer, white houses
set back from the road. The man whom the boy has come
to collect from shuffles onto the porch. As is his custom,
he wears a gray dress with flowers. Long gray hair
covers his shoulders, catches in a week's growth of beard.
The boy opens the door and glancing down he sees yellow
streaks of urine running down the man's legs, snaking
into the gray socks and loafers. For a year, the boy
has delivered the man's papers, mowed and raked his lawn.
He's even been inside the house which stinks of excrement
and garbage, with forgotten bags of groceries on tables:
rotten fruit, moldy bread, packages of unopened hamburger.
He would wait in the hall as the man counted out pennies
from a paper bag, adding five extra out of kindness.
The boy thinks of when the man's mother was alive.
He would sneak up to the house when the music began
and watch the man and his mother dance cheek to cheek
around the kitchen, slowly, hesitantly, as if each
thought the other could break as simply as a china plate.
The mother had been dead a week when a neighbor found her
and even then her son wouldn't let her go. The boy sat

on the curb watching the man hurl his fat body against
the immaculate state troopers who tried not to touch him
but only keep him from where men from the funeral home
carried out his mother wrapped in red blankets, smelling
like hamburger left for weeks on the umbrella stand.

Today as the boy waits on the top step watching the urine
trickle into the man's socks, he raises his head to see
the pale blue eyes fixed upon him with their wrinkles and
bags and zigzagging red lines. As he stares into them,
he begins to believe he is staring out of those eyes,
looking down at a thin blond boy on his front steps.
Then he lifts his head and still through the man's eyes
he sees the softness of late afternoon light on the street
where the man has spent his entire life, sees the green
of summer, white Victorian houses as through a white fog
so they shimmer and flicker before him. Looking past
the houses, past the first fields, he sees the reddening
sky of sunset, sees the land rushing west as if it wanted
to smash itself as completely as a cup thrown to the floor,
violently pursuing the sky with great spirals of red wind.

Abruptly the boy steps back. When he looks again into
the man's eyes, they appear bottomless and sad; and he
wants to touch his arm, say he's sorry about his mother,
sorry he's crazy, sorry he lets urine run down his leg
and wears a dress. Instead, he gives him his paper
and leaves. As he raises his bike, he looks out toward
red sky and darkening earth, and they seem poised
like two animals that have always hated each other,
each fiercely wanting to tear out the other's throat:
black dog, red dog— now more despairing, more resolved.

What You Have Come to Expect

The worn plush of the seat chafes your bare legs
as you shiver in the air-conditioned dark
watching a man embrace his wife at the edge

of their shadowy lawn. It is just past dusk
and behind them their house rises white and
symmetrical. Candles burn in each window,
while from the open door a blade of light jabs
down the gravel path to a fountain. In the doorway
wait two children dressed for sleep in white gowns.
The man touches his wife's cheek. Although
he must leave, he is frightened for her safety and
the safety of their children. At last he hurries
to where two horses stamp and whinny in harness.
Then, from your seat in the third row, you follow him
through battles and bloodshed and friends lost
until finally he returns home: rides up the lane
as dusk falls to discover all that remains of his house
is a single chimney rising from ashes and mounds of debris.
Where is his young wife? He stares out across
empty fields, the wreckage of stables and barns.
Where are the children who were the comfort of his life?

In a few minutes, you plunge into the brilliant light
of the afternoon sun. Across the street, you see your bike
propped against a wall with your dog waiting beside it.
The dog is so excited to see you she keeps leaping up,
licking your face, while you, still full of the movie,
full of its colors and music and lives sacrificed to some
heroic purpose, try to tell her about this unutterable
sadness you feel on a Saturday afternoon in July 1950.
Bicycling home, you keep questioning what happened
to the children, what happened to their father standing
by the burned wreckage of his house, and you wish
there were someone to explain this problem to, someone
to help you understand this sense of bereavement and loss:
you, who are too young even to regret the passage of time.
Next year your favorite aunt will die, then your
grandparents, one by one, then even your cousins.
You sit on the seat of your green bike with balloon tires
and watch your dog waiting up the street: a Bayeux
tapestry dog, brindle with thin legs and a greyhound chest,
a dog now no more than a speck of ash in the Michigan dirt.
From a distance of thirty years, you see yourself paused

at the intersection: a thin blond boy in khaki shorts;
see yourself push off into the afternoon sunlight,
clumsily entering your future the way a child urged on
by its frightened nurse might stumble into a plowed field
in the dead of night: half running, half pulled along.
Behind them: gunshots, flame and the crack of burning wood.
Far ahead: a black line of winter trees.

Now, after thirty years, the trees have come closer.
Glancing around you, you discover you are alone;
raising your hands to your face and beard, you find
you are no longer young, while the only fires
are in the fleck of stars above you, the only face
is the crude outline of the moon's: distant, as any family
you might have had; cold, in a way you have come to expect.

The Gun

Late afternoon light slices through the dormer window
to your place on the floor next to a stack of comics.
Across from you is a boy who at eleven is three years
older. He is telling you to pull down your pants.
You tell him you don't want to. His mother is out
and you are alone in the house. He has given you a Coke,
let you smoke two of his mother's nonfilter Pall Malls,
and years later you can still picture the red packet
on the dark finish of the phonograph. You stand up
and say you have to go home. You live across the street
and only see him in summer when he returns from school.
As you step around the comics toward the stairs,
the boy gives you a shove, sends you stumbling back.
Wait, he says, I want to show you something.
He goes to a drawer and when he turns around
you see he is holding a small gun by the barrel.
You feel you are breathing glass. You ask if it is
loaded and he says, Sure it is, and you say: Show me.
He removes the clip, takes a bullet from his pocket.
See this, he says, then puts the bullet into the clip,

slides the clip into the butt of the gun with a snap.
The boy sits on the bed and pretends to study the gun.
He has a round fat face and black hair. Take off
your pants, he says. Again you say you have to go home.
He stands up and points the gun at your legs. Slowly,
you unhook your cowboy belt, undo the metal buttons
of your jeans. They slide down past your knees.
Pull down your underwear, he tells you. You tell him
you don't want to. He points the gun at your head.
You crouch on the floor, cover your head with your hands.
You don't want him to see you cry. You feel you are
pulling yourself into yourself and soon you will be
no bigger than a pebble. You think back to the time
you saw a friend's cocker spaniel hit by a car and you
remember how its stomach was split open and you imagine
your face split open and blood and gray stuff escaping.
You have hardly ever thought of dying, seriously dying,
and as you grow more scared you have to go to the bathroom
more and more badly. Before you can stop yourself,
you feel yourself pissing into your underwear.
The boy with the gun sees the spreading pool of urine.
You baby, he shouts, you baby, you're disgusting.
You want to apologize, but the words jumble and
choke in your throat. Get out, the boy shouts.
You drag your pants up over your wet underwear and
run down the stairs. As you slam out of his house,
you know you died up there among the comic books
and football pennants, died as sure as your friend's
cocker spaniel, as sure as if the boy had shot your
face off, shot the very piss out of you. Standing
in the street with urine soaking your pants, you watch
your neighbors pursuing the orderly occupations
of a summer afternoon: mowing a lawn, trimming a hedge.
Where is that sense of the world you woke with
this morning? Now it is smaller. Now it has gone away.

General Matthei Drives Home Through Santiago

The part where General Matthei leaves his office,
I don't know about. And when he gets home,
that I don't know about either. Or if he had
a hard day or an easy day or if his secretary
bent down in front of him so he could see her
large breasts or if he has a secretary or if she has breasts—
all this remains shrouded in mystery. Likewise,
when he got home, whether his four Dobermans
romped out to greet him or if he spent his evening
polishing his pistolas— this too is hidden from me.
But I know for certain it takes twelve men to help
General Matthei drive home; it takes five vehicles:
two motorcycles with sirens and three big gray cars.
Were they Mercedes? They were going too fast to tell.
As for why it is necessary for him to hurry home
so rapidly, this too is a mystery, except
that each day he requires twelve men, five vehicles
and most of the speed in Santiago. It has been said
his bowels were shot away in a duel and the poor general
must spend his life rushing from bathroom to bathroom.
It has been said that as general of the air force
he fears the earth as the wealthy fear the poor.
Or perhaps he is jealous of his wife or has bread
baking in the oven or is accustomed to watching
the American cartoons on the TV at seven-thirty.
But the other generals of the Junta also rush home
at 100 kilometers per hour down the crowded avenidas.
Surely they are not all jealous of their wives.
So again the curtain of mystery is lowered before us.
But yesterday as I was driving home and the general
was driving home and about a million other residents
of Santiago were also going home, I saw the small
humiliation of a middle-aged woman in a small red Fiat
who was neither beautiful, nor was she driving fast.
Maybe she was thinking about her dinner or maybe
her car radio was turned up and she was singing

to the music. In any case, she didn't hear the sirens.
The military policeman riding the first motorcycle
wore white leather gauntlets that nearly reached
his elbows, and when the red Fiat had the audacity
not to scramble for the curb, he swerved around it
and smashed his fist down hard on the red Fiat's hood.
For an instant, that was the loudest noise in Santiago.
Did the red Fiat leap several feet in the air?
I believe it did. Then it braked and swerved right and
dozens of other cars braked and swerved right and blew
their horns and in that moment the general was gone.
I wish I could say all this led to some small tragedy—
that the red Fiat smashed the cart of a man selling bread
or ran over a dog or the woman swallowed her teeth.
But this was a very normal evening in late spring and the sky
was as blue as ever and the lowering sun had just begun
to redden the tips of the snow-capped Andes and in another
moment the tangled cars straightened themselves out
and the woman in the red Fiat simply drove home.
When she arrived, maybe she told her husband about
the general and maybe he went out and stared at the Fiat
but saw nothing but a smear in the dust on the red hood.
But maybe he looked at it and the rest of his family
looked at it and maybe he mentioned it to some friends
and they looked at it too. And someday when General Matthei
is shot and dragged by his heels through the streets,
this man will think of his red Fiat and suck his teeth
and, in a way that is typical of the people of Santiago,
he will half roll and half shrug one of his shoulders
as if letting a heavy strap at last slide from it.

WAYNE DODD

Outside My Cabin

now the birds
are talking softly

among themselves,
supper over, their shoes off,

the woods darkening and lights
coming on in the little houses.

Comfort the voices say.
It's been a long day

they answer, trusting, drowsy,
the trees swaying gently

in the wind, somebody's husband
or wife already losing

the rhythm, the breathing
becoming labored,

irregular, tomorrow
as distant as China.

Letter

All the pages inside me are blank.

I have not seen strawberries in a high meadow
For how many seasons?

Now the chipmunks are thin
And restless in their sleep.

Friend, what I need today is one clear message
I can send

And receive.

Like Deer Our Bodies

All the way home the ground
Fog rises and swirls

Around us, snow turning to air
As we breathe, as we drive

This familiar road
Back through February

Home. Houses, whole hillsides of
Trees bulk beside us, seen

Only in memory.
Like deer our bodies,

Silent together in secret
Grass, do not

Speak but dream
Still, beneath the hovering

Cold, of food
And ease among friends. Soon

Together we will sleep once more
Our separate lives. And when

Tomorrow at first light we
Wake, each

Branch and blade on
Peach Ridge Road will flash

New ice: fog
Remembered, fog saved.

Weathering Out

She liked mornings the best— Thomas gone
to look for work, her coffee flushed with milk,

outside autumn trees blowsy and dripping.
Past the seventh month she couldn't see her feet

so she floated from room to room, houseshoes flapping,
navigating corners in wonder. When she leaned

against a door jamb to yawn, she disappeared entirely.

Last week they had taken a bus at dawn
to the new airdock. The hangar slid open in segments

and the zeppelin nosed forward in its silver envelope.
The man walked it out gingerly, like a poodle,

then tied it to a mast and went back inside.
Beulah felt just that large and placid, a lake;

she glistened from cocoa butter smoothed in
when Thomas returned every evening nearly

in tears. He'd lean an ear on her belly
and say: *Little fellow's really talking,*

though to her it was more the *pok-pok-pok*
of a fingernail tapping a thick cream lampshade.

Sometimes during the night she woke and found him
asleep there and the child sleeping, too.

The coffee was good but too little. Outside
everything shivered in tinfoil— only the clover

between the cobblestones hung stubbornly on,
green as an afterthought . . .

The Event

Ever since they'd left the Tennessee ridge
with nothing to boast of
but good looks and a mandolin,

the two Negroes leaning
on the rail of a riverboat
were inseparable: Lem plucked

to Thomas' silver falsetto.
But the night was hot and they were drunk.
They spat where the wheel

churned mud and moonlight,
they called to the tarantulas
down among the bananas

to come out and dance.
*You're so fine and mighty; let's see
what you can do*, said Thomas, pointing

to a tree-capped island.
Lem stripped, spoke easy: *Them's chestnuts,
I believe*. Dove

quick as a gasp. Thomas, dry
on deck, saw the green crown shake
as the island slipped

under, dissolved
in the thickening stream.
At his feet

a stinking circle of rags,
the half-shell mandolin.
Where the wheel turned the water

gently shirred.

Parsley

1. The Cane Fields

There is a parrot imitating spring
in the palace, its feathers parsley green.
Out of the swamp the cane appears

to haunt us, and we cut it down. El General
searches for a word; he is all the world
there is. Like a parrot imitating spring,

we lie down screaming as rain punches through
and we come up green. We cannot speak an R—
out of the swamp, the cane appears

and then the mountain we call in whispers *Katalina*.
The children gnaw their teeth to arrowheads.
There is a parrot imitating spring.

El General has found his word: *perejil*.
Who says it, lives. He laughs, teeth shining
out of the swamp. The cane appears

in our dreams, lashed by wind and streaming.
And we lie down. For every drop of blood
there is a parrot imitating spring.
Out of the swamp the cane appears.

2. The Palace

The word the general's chosen is parsley.
It is fall, when thoughts turn

to love and death; the general thinks
of his mother, how she died in the fall
and he planted her walking cane at the grave
and it flowered, each spring stolidly forming
four-star blossoms. The general

pulls on his boots, he stomps to
her room in the palace, the one without
curtains, the one with a parrot
in a brass ring. As he paces he wonders
Who can I kill today. And for a moment
the little knot of screams
is still. The parrot, who has traveled

all the way from Australia in an ivory
cage, is, coy as a widow, practising
spring. Ever since the morning
his mother collapsed in the kitchen
while baking skull-shaped candies
for the Day of the Dead, the general
has hated sweets. He orders pastries
brought up for the bird; they arrive

dusted with sugar on a bed of lace.
The knot in his throat starts to twitch;
he sees his boots the first day in battle
splashed with mud and urine
as a soldier falls at his feet amazed—
how stupid he looked!—at the sound
of artillery. *I never thought it would sing*
the soldier said, and died. Now

the general sees the fields of sugar
cane, lashed by rain and streaming.
He sees his mother's smile, the teeth
gnawed to arrowheads. He hears
the Haitians sing without R's
as they swing the great machetes:
Katalina, they sing, *Katalina*,

mi madle, mi amol en muelte. God knows
his mother was no stupid woman; she
could roll an R like a queen. Even
a parrot can roll an R! In the bare room
the bright feathers arch in a parody
of greenery, as the last pale crumbs
disappear under the blackened tongue. Someone

calls out his name in a voice
so like his mother's, a startled tear
splashes the tip of his right boot.
My mother, my love in death.
The general remembers the tiny green sprigs
men of his village wore in their capes
to honor the birth of a son. He will
order many, this time, to be killed

for a single, beautiful word.

The Bird Frau

When the boys came home, everything stopped
the way he left it—her apron, the back stairs,
the sun losing altitude over France
as the birds scared up from the fields,
a whirring curtain of flak—

                    Barmherzigkeit!
her son, her man. She went inside, fed the parakeet,
broke its neck. Spaetzle bubbling on the stove,
windchimes tinkling above the steam, her face
in the hall mirror, bloated, a heart.
Let everything go wild!

                    Blue jays, crows!
She hung suet from branches, the air quick
around her head with tiny spastic machinery
—starlings, finches—her head a crown of feathers.

She ate less, grew lighter, air tunnelling
through bone, singing

                  a small song.
"Ein Liedchen, Kinder!" The children ran away.
She moved about the yard like an old rag bird.
Still at war, she rose at dawn, watching out
for Rudi, come home on crutches,
the thin legs balancing his atom of life.

Geometry

I prove a theorem and the house expands:
the windows jerk free to hover near the ceiling,
the ceiling floats away with a sigh.

As the walls clear themselves of everything
but transparency, the scent of carnations
leaves with them. I am out in the open

and above the windows have hinged into butterflies,
sunlight glinting where they've intersected.
They are going to some point true and unproven.

Stephen Dunn

Let's See If I Have It Right

I kiss these before I kiss that,
then I wait to see
if you're the kind who'll kiss this.
If you're not I go on kissing
these and that, careful always
to place my hands where my lips
are not. However, if you do kiss this

I can choose to lie back
and watch or arrange myself
in such a way so I can kiss that
while you're kissing this so that
kissing is no longer the exact word.
Around this time, as I recall,
every part of speech is ready
for every other part, whether it speaks
or not, and that and sometimes
the other thing is entered by this
with its single accurate eye
and *still* there are various options
and contingencies which (it is said)
I will remember before the time comes
for this to come or that kingdom
of yours to come, and I think
I'm allowed to touch these
if I can reach them, which always
is supposed to depend.

The Routine Things Around the House

When mother died
I thought: now I'll have a death poem.
That was unforgivable

yet I've since forgiven myself
as sons are able to do
who've been loved by their mothers.

I stared into the coffin
knowing how long she'd live,
how many lifetimes there are

in the sweet revisions of memory.
It's hard to know exactly
how we ease ourselves back from sadness,

but I remembered when I was twelve,
1951, before the world
unbuttoned its blouse.

I had asked my mother (I was trembling)
if I could see her breasts
and she took me into her room

without embarrassment or coyness
and I stared at them,
afraid to ask for more.

Now, years later, someone tells me
Cancers who've never had mother love
are doomed and I, a Cancer,

feel blessed again. What luck
to have had a mother
who showed me her breasts

when girls my age were developing
their separate countries,
what luck

she didn't doom me
with too much or too little.
Had I asked to touch,

perhaps to suck them,
what would she have done?
Mother, dead woman

who I think permits me
to love women easily,
this poem

is dedicated to where
we stopped, to the incompleteness
that was sufficient

and to how you buttoned up,
began doing the routine things
around the house.

Essay on the Personal

Because finally the personal
is all that matters,
we spend years describing stones,
chairs, abandoned farm houses—
until we're ready. Always
it's a matter of precision,
what it feels like
to kiss someone or to walk
out the door. How good it was
to practice on stones
which were things we could love
without weeping over. How good
someone else abandoned the farm house,
bankrupt and desperate.
Now we can bring a fine edge
to our parents. We can hold hurt
up to the sun for examination.
But just when we think we have it,
the personal goes the way of
belief. What seemed so deep
begins to seem naïve, something
that could be trusted
because we hadn't read Plato
or held two contradictory ideas
or women in the same day.
Love, then, becomes an old movie.
Loss seems so common
it belongs to the air,
to breath itself, anyone's.
We're left with style, a particular
way of standing and saying,
the idiosyncratic look
at the frown which means nothing

until we say it does. Years later,
long after we believed it peculiar
to ourselves, we return to love.
We return to everything
strange, inchoate, like living
with someone, like living alone,
settling for the partial, the almost
satisfactory sense of it.

Truck Stop: Minnesota

The waitress looks at my face
as if it were a small tip.
I'm tempted to come back at her
with *java*
but I say *coffee*, politely,
and tell her how I want it.
Her body has the alert sleepiness
of a cat's. Her face
the indecency of a billboard.
She is the America I would like to love.
Sweetheart, the truckers call her.
Honey. Doll.
For each of them, she smiles.
I envy them,
I'm full of lust and good usage,
lost here.
I imagine every man she's left with
has smelled of familiar food,
has peppered her with wild slang
until she was damp and loose.
I do nothing but ask for a check
and drift out into the night air—
let my dreams lift
her tired feet off the ground
into the sweet, inarticulate
democracy beyond my ears—
and keep moving until I'm home
in the middle of my country.

Desire

I remember how it used to be
at noon, springtime, the city streets
full of office workers like myself
let loose from the cold
glass buildings on Park and Lex,
the dull swaddling of winter cast off,
almost everyone wanting
everyone else. It was amazing
how most of us contained ourselves,
bringing desire back up
to the office where it existed anyway,
quiet, like a good engine.
I'd linger a bit
with the receptionist,
knock on someone else's open door,
ease myself, by increments,
into the seriousness they paid me for.
Desire was everywhere those years,
so enormous it couldn't be reduced
one person at a time.
I don't remember when it was,
though closer to now than then,
I walked the streets desireless,
my eyes fixed on destination alone.
The beautiful person across from me
on the bus or train
looked like effort, work.
I translated her into pain.
For months I had the clarity
the cynical survive with,
their world so safely small.
Today, walking 57th toward 3rd,
it's all come back,
the interesting, the various,
the conjured life suggested by a glance.
I praise how the body heals itself.
I praise how, finally, it never learns.

CORNELIUS EADY

The Supremes

We were born to be gray. We went to school,
Sat in rows, ate white bread,
Looked at the floor a lot. In the back
Of our small heads

A long scream. We did what we could,
And all we could do was
Turn on each other. How the fat kids suffered!
Not even being jolly could save them.

And then there were the anal retentives,
The terrified brown-noses, the desperately
Athletic or popular. This, of course,
Was training. At home

Our parents shook their heads and waited.
We learned of the industrial revolution,
The sectioning of the clock into pie slices.
We drank Cokes and twiddled our thumbs. In the
Back of our minds

A long scream. We snapped butts in the showers,
Froze out shy girls on the dance floor,
Pin-pointed flaws like radar.
Slowly we understood: this was to be the world.

We were born insurance salesmen and secretaries,
Housewives and short order cooks,
Stock room boys and repairmen,
And it wouldn't be a bad life, they promised,
In a tone of voice that would force some of us
To reach in self-defense for wigs,
Lipstick,

Sequins.

Young Elvis

He's driving a truck, and we know
What he knows: His sweat
And hips move the wrong product.
In Memphis, behind a thick
Pane of glass, a stranger daydreams

Of a voice as tough as a Negro's,
But not a Negro's. A voice that
Slaps instead of *twangs*,
But not a Negro's. When it
Struts through the door
(Like he knows it will), and
Opens up, rides

The spiky strings of
The guitar, pushes
The bass line below the belt,
Reveals the drums
As cheap pimps,
In fact transforms the whole proceedings
Into a cat house, a lost night . . .

He wets his lips.
Already the young driver is imagining
A 20th century birthday present,
The one-shot lark of his recorded voice,
The awe he intends to
Shine through his mother's favorite hymns.

Sherbet

The problem here is that
This isn't pretty, the
Sort of thing which

Can easily be dealt with
With words. After
All it's

A horror story to sit,
A black man with
A white wife in

The middle of a hot
Sunday afternoon at
The Jefferson Hotel in

Richmond, VA, and wait
Like a criminal for service
From a young white waitress

Who has decided that
This looks like something
She doesn't want

To be a part of. What poetry
Could describe the
Perfect angle of

This woman's back as
She walks, just so,
Mapping the room off

Like the end of a
Border dispute, which
Metaphor could turn

The room more perfectly
Into a group of
Islands? And when

The manager finally
Arrives, what language
Do I use

To translate the nervous
Eye motions, the yawning
Afternoon silence, the

Prayer beneath
His simple inquiries,
The sherbet which

He then brings to the table personally,
Just to be certain
The doubt

Stays on our side
Of the fence? What do
We call the rich,

Sweet taste of
Frozen oranges in
This context? What do

We call a weight that
Doesn't fingerprint,
Won't shift

And can't explode?

Thrift

What happens when an old black man,
Toothless and raggedy,
Walks into a bank, catches
Some young, white, middle-manager's ear
With a slurred tale of coins
Hoarded from his wife and kids
(Who would only have spent them),
Leftovers from various hits
On the numbers, plus

God knows how many
Easy deceptions.

If you were this man, what
Would you do with this true believer
Who has walked through the door
Of your bank, fired up
With what he has pulled off,
Knowing that on some non-verbal level
He has encoded you
(Or someone like you)

As kindred, that only you
(Or someone like you)
Could understand this type
Of fidelity. And somehow
He guides you to the door
And through the glass you see
The trunk of this man's car,
My father's car, its springs
Low and ripe as the apricots
Sweetening on his tree
At home. He wants to give you

The weight he has built, penny
By penny. He wants you to lift
Away what you first thought of him,
Bag by precious bag. And he wants
You to do it, now.

LYNN EMANUEL

Patient

I remember my grandmother on her hard knees
Complaining to the floor about the rich,

Her voice rough across the slick rise
Of their culpabilities and her hand moving

From the mouth of the zinc bucket
To the floor beside the bed where I

Watched, sick, waiting for the cold kiss
of salt and wet bread. She fed me that damp

White lump on a tarnished spoon
While the long limousines

Climbed the tipped hill to the house
Where a man my grandmother loved

Shared the bright empty plate of the table
With his wife. At night my grandmother

Would lie small and white
As an egg in an apron, silent as the snake

Laying its green throat on the pillow
Of the walk. She thought about him until

His face was a moth wing worn away
By the soft curiosity of a child.

What Grieving Was Like

That was not the summer of aspic
and cold veal. It was so hot

the car seat stung my thighs
and the rear view mirror swam

with mirage. In the back seat
the leather grip was noosed by twine.

We were not poor but we had
the troubles of the poor.

She who had been that soft snore
beside the Nytol, open-mouthed,

was gone, somewhere, somewhere
there was bay, there was a boat,

there was a scold in mother's mouth.
What I remember best

is the way everything came and went
in the window of my brief attention.

At the wake I was beguiled
by the chromium yellow lemon pies.

The grandfather clock's pendant
of unaffordable gold told the quarter hour.

The hearse rolled forward over the O's
of its own surprise.

Self-Portrait at Eighteen

Today I became my own secret admirer, unearthing
from the junk—the boxes of napkins tatted by grandmother
and Great Aunt Tiny, the cobwebby bulk of table linens
that covered the scab of scratched deal that was their kitchen
table where they gave thanks and passed the faded confetti
of the succotash—this photograph. It is not a flash of family
dinner, but a luminous window, the faded wash of clouds
strung up in Talamone. Somewhere at the rim a somewhat
    darker,
rumpled mass of—what?—the photographer's jacket, or the
    blanket

where, after buying two tabs of acid from a boy who sold
a handful along the shore, we made love and then set out to
sabotage, respectability or, at least in my case, self-regard.
In the foreground a fringe of reeds suggests the landscape
blinked at this girl-stretched-naked-on-the-sand,
although *stretched* implies, passivity, loss of will and clearly
this is a willful, though awkward abandonment, an act
of exposure not merely meant but mutinous. Uncanny
the resemblance of the pose—awkward, although not
     innocent—
to an inexperienced lounge singer, maybe a girl leaning
uneasily against a black piano; she has knuckled under
to convention but clearly not enough or generously.
Still, I love the delicate bones of my pelvis, (the bony repose
that suggests, as well, the sculptures on sarcophagi)
in this photograph which a not-quite-forgotten-enough
photographer entitled: Portrait of a Woman, Nude.

Ruth Fainlight

Stubborn

My Stone-Age self still scorns
attempts to prove us more
than upright animals
whose powerful skeletons
and sinewy muscled limbs
were made to be exhausted
by decades of labour
not subdued by thought,

despises still those dreamers
who forget, poets
who ignore, heroes
who defy mortality

while risking every failure,
spirits unsatisfied
by merely their own
bodily survival.

I know her awful strength.
I know how panic, envy,
self-defense, are mixed
with her tormented rage
because they will deny
her argument that nothing
but the body's pleasure,
use, and comfort, matters.

Guarding her cave and fire
and implements, stubborn
in her ignorance,
deaf to all refutation,
I know she must insist
until the hour of death
she cannot feel the pain
that shapes and haunts me.

Spring in the City

Petals from the trees
along the street
revolve and fall.
Complex currents
lift them up toward
the boughs from which
their flight was launched.

All the space between
the rows of houses
in swirling movement
like sand in a rock-pool

as the sea sluices through
raising fine clouds
that blur its clearness.

Gutters choked with blossom
pavements patterned
the wind-blown hair of girls
tangled with blossom
a swarm of insects
aquarium of fishes
snowflakes in a storm.

Shaken by the breeze
and cornering cars
reaffirming the spiral
of the galaxies
the air today seems thick
with stardust and we
are breathing stars.

The Future

The future is timid and wayward
and wants to be courted, will not
respond to threats or coaxing,
and hears excuses only
when she feels secure.

Doubt, uproar, jeers,
vengeful faces roughened
by angry tears, the harsh
odours of self-importance,
are what alarm her most.

Nothing you do will lure her
from the corner where
she waits like a nun of a closed

order or a gifted young
dancer, altogether

the creature of her vocation,
with those limits and strengths.
Trying to reassure her,
find new alibis
and organize the proof

of your enthrallment and
devotion, seems totally useless—
though it teaches how
to calm your spirit, move
beyond the problem's overt

cause and one solution—
until the future, soothed now,
starts to plot another
outcome to the story:
your difficult reward.

CHARLES FORT

The Worker (We Own Two Houses)

My father was a barber-surgeon
for thirty-three years
and a factory worker
for eighteen of those years.

On Saturdays it seemed as if
the entire Negro section of town
had grown long hair.
The sounds of shears

still vibrate my ears.
I swept clouds into the wastebasket.
The back room contained hard whiskey
bookies and hidden magazines.

When my father came home at seven a.m.
lifting his black aluminum lunch box,
we seven children met him at the door,
knelt, and untied his shoes.
His tired eyes burned lines
into the side of that box.
Each of us wanted left-overs;
we grew older and took turns.
Steel ball-bearings turned in his hands,
given to us as marbles
and the largest on the block.

They made my father a supervisor;
his white friends for eighteen years
now turned from his voice.
Years before the Army
broke his legs in basic training,
fused them for life.

When dust began to fill my father's bones,
I learned how chronic arthritis
can lock together any old man.
From the back room I heard my name
and a razor being slapped against leather.
With magazines thrown into place
I carried out his clean towels.
I picked up clouds.

How Old Are the People of the World

They are scattered ageless souls
urging the minutes and hours to cease,
mere shadows in their aching slumber

rising like temples born out of fire.
They are blind survivors traveling primitive waters
rescued from the only god they knew
by a child willing to ask how old
are the people of the world, a child able
to see how twilight releases its carpentry:
yesterday the stars were gold coins spinning to earth.
They are shapes thrown together by the rattled eye
driven like a memory lost in its own fever,
telling as a town crier flying death's carriage
drawn into the belly pool of time.
It is winter becoming winter again.
Blue fog cuts the tops of trees,
dispersed, October, still moving
unrelenting as eyes searching out food
as the man to first raise his hand for blood
kicking the locust for its very idea.

The Town Clock Burning

This clock positions each of us
in one square block behind the church.
Nothing has counted more and year after year
we march as it tells us to march.

This half-sleeping clock falters.
Its pendulum craves motion and time.
As powder and flame shadow each face
we guard what it tells us to guard.

Does this half-stepping helmsman
know how a holy war begins?
What bell shaped terror?   What moan?   What hour
we stop when it tells us to stop?

This is the clock of boundaries
marking its descent as its final seconds
pass into history and without pause
we harm what it tells us to harm.

BRENDAN GALVIN

Willow, Wishbone, Warblers

The way this willow traps
fallen branches till it looks like
a collapsed rookery,
and keeps sun out of this room,

and taps the vegetables' water,
fattening on vitamins
so it's taller than the house now,
and, come March, won't put out

many catkins— but for the enchantment
of a single branch bobbing on air
after some winged departure,
I'd take a saw to it.

The trunk and limbs would make fenceposts
for the garden, or in the fireplace
hold off a few winter evenings,
and the branches could supply

years of beanpoles tall enough
so the tendrils could work out
any Book of Kells design they had
in mind. Mainly it's the birds, though,

all those minute fussings in its
leaves, calls and their seedy replies,
convincing me, August through September,
that I'm simpler than I think,

a gawper at flutterings down the trunk
though I've vowed to lock up

the field glasses, not to look this year
when immature warblers that won't stay put

long enough to be anything
run their mirroring duets like air shows
around the trees, and far out on the bay,
flocks go stringing over water

in lines that falter and break to flecks
and lift again on their wishbones
beyond all but a suggestion of birds
backlit by evening, beyond even

my intuition of their cries, and I praise
the fact beneath superstition's skin:
that bone we go dowsing for luck with,
there like a small horseshoe stamped in.

Chickadee

The crow is only an anvil,
and the goldfinches' song
can be duplicated by rubbing
the right sticks together.
Next to yours
the blue feet of titmice
are merely a fad.

There are jays with voices
full of elbows
in my world, too,
dragoons on leave,
who appear to have molted
all the way to their head points.

But you, minimal wingbeat,
you're there, not there:
the economy of your arrival

puts a whole squad
of evening grosbeaks to shame.

I believe that other puritan
was looking at you when
he first thought, "Beware of
enterprises that require
new clothes."

I've believed in your way
since that evening
the owl sat
waiting for light to drain
into dusk, and you
flew straight in

and, seeing him there,
at the last instant
dipped up just enough,
and taught me
the duende of chickadees.

Seals in the Inner Harbor

Ducks, at first, except they didn't
fly when we rounded the jetty
and swung into the channel,
didn't spread panic among themselves,
peeling the whole flock off the water,
but followed, popping under
and poking up as if to study our faces
for someone, their eyes rounded still
by the first spearing shock of ice,
or amazed to find our white town
here again, backed by a steeple
telling the hours in sea time.
Their skeptical brows seemed from a day
when men said a green Christmas

would fill this harbor with dead
by February. We left them hanging
astern at world's edge, afloat on
summer's afterlife: gray jetty,
water and sky, the one gray vertical
of smoke rising straight from a chimney
across the cove. We could believe
they were men who had dragged
this bottom till its shells were smooth
and round as gift shop wampum,
who never tied up and walked away
a final time, but returned for evenings
like this was going to be, thirsting
for something to fight salt off with,
needing a place to spit and plan
the rescue of children's children.

Listening to September

In this season of brief arrivals
and long departures,
when light and shade meander
through these pines
slow as Holsteins, I spend
an afternoon turning things
upside down to see whether
arrowheads or train-flattened
pennies fall out. Those new
whistlers back there in the trees
sound like kids calling a dog
in their private way,
though I know they are only
birds, or only memory
like time burrowing in
ledge over ledge, dovetailing,
holding on. When they were kids,
men I used to know
herded cows here, after

the oaks fell for ships and
their business, before pines
parceled the river out
to pools backing their stands.
No houses this side, only
treeless pasture then,
and though those whistlers
may be warblers I've never seen,
passing through, I don't
want to spot them
for my list just now.

Town Pier Parking Lot

From the time we were caught up
in its drawn-out, shallow
flight dips and the way it used
masts for an overview, its silhouette
shifting like a wind pennant,
then dived, and flew to a crosstree
to swallow the catch, we must have
followed that kingfisher half an hour.
I was too tricked out in my new ego
to see events like this when I was
a kid here, my eyes so slicked over
with self I used to think
those couples who'd park at the pier
an evening and just sit still
were busybodies or so bored that
a dragger off-loading or fish truck's
departure for Boston was a thrill.
I was streamlined with talk then,
and they seemed already cracked
and peeling, but now that we're
nearly the age they were and can
call them by their Christian names,
I see how the world waits for us
to warp to its weathers and need it,

sends from its least places
a kingfisher, or in winter, as fog
takes the breakwater and draggers,
a heron flying in, just blue enough
to be separate from fog.

GARY GILDNER

Cabbage in Polish

Cabbage in Polish is kapusta— ka*poo*sta.
Street is ulica— oo*leet*sa.
                              Our street,
Ulica Staffa, is named for a poet,
Leopold Staff (the extra *a* means possession).
To honor our luck, and his, we have invented
two dishes: cabbage leaves neatly wrapped
around meat, called Kapusta Staffa Stuffa,
and a cabbage-and-meat concoction, all chopped up,
called Kapusta Staffa Loosa.
The latter results when the former fails.
This little ditty intends to say nothing more,
contains no hidden meanings, no subtle
references to freedom, madness, or long delays in jails.
The rhymes are only goofy, like stuffed cabbages
that end in a mess. Give them a good name,
eat them, brush the crumbs away, and slip off to bed.
Steal a kiss. Dream your dreams. Don't forget.

String

The women in the Polish P.O.—their clusters
of bunched-up consonants exploding
and ricocheting off the walls like so many Chinese
firecrackers—sent me reeling in the dark
with my three mailers of books back and forth

between the two stations they commanded,
until this hard fact slowly shone through:
neither woman wanted me: my mailers
were too big for one, and for the other
I had no string around them—string
being essential, required by law, without it
everything would fall apart during the journey
and then where would I be? said the string woman,
who moved her pretty Slavic fingers with such nimble
and lacy grace to help me understand this impossible
situation, that I now felt something like the fuzzy
combustions of love burning under my scalp.
I needed to respond somehow, to show her
this time everything was different, not to fret,
that what I'd laid on her scales was tough as nails.
So getting a good grip on my biggest American-
made mailer and then dipping into the classic, slowly
uncoiling crouch that discus throwers have burst from
since the beginning, I flung the unstrung thing up, up
and away, toward the Gothic rafters of that Polish P. O.
Oh, it flew and flew and no one at that moment
could have been more possessed by his power
than I was, and when it almost reached
where no man would ever dream to touch,
I began to reflect on a law I never had much use for
—i.e., objects in motion tend to remain in motion.
I didn't believe it in my youth when all smacked
baseballs and all spun-off hubcaps soon stopped dead
in the weeds somewhere, and I didn't much trust it now
watching my discus-mailer of hardbound books, run out of
gas and glory, begin its heavy, necessary journey
down from the ceiling, toward a tiny, ancient, white-
haired grandma, who sat, composed as porcelain,
at a table, writing; surely she had come in
from the cold with only one thing in mind:
to send sweet wishes and high hopes for many
healthy tomorrows to her loved ones far away—in Puck
perhaps, or Lódz—for indeed it was Christmas week

and who among us wants to hear about misery.
I saw myself hauled off by the Milicja,
and I saw the headline: American Brains Innocent Babcia.
They'd throw the book at me, of course, I deserved it,
a hot-headed Yankee off his nut. And no nice poppyseed
cakes, no piwo, no luscious pierogi stuffed
with cheese, meat, or creamy potatoes where I was going—
And then my mailer came down with a great whack
to the floor, landing inches from the little babcia's feet.
Slowly she raised her eyes and regarded it,
then around till she found me,
then back to her writing as if the flat brown thing
and the man gripping his hair didn't exist,
that nothing in fact had happened— or if it had,
so what, she had seen bigger noises fall from the sky.
My fires were out, cold; it was time to pick up and go.
Turning to the other two women, I saw that
they had somehow gotten together
and were blushing, blushing like impossible peaches!
And pulling dozens of loose strings out of nowhere.

"Primarily We Miss Ourselves As Children"

— a Warsaw student, overheard

I miss the toad poking up in the mud.
I miss mistaking the mud for the toad.
I am now in a house in Poland, I had
oatmeal for breakfast, I had oatmeal for breakfast
in America, in 1942. I was late for school.
Brownie my collie followed me to school.
I sat in a circle, I slept on a rug.
I smelled milk on my fingers, brown pieces of mud.

Go to sleep now, Gary, go to sleep, go to sleep
and when you wake up we'll be at the farm.
The long road to get there, counting telephone poles.
Szostak, Szostak was my grandfather's name,

he lay his head on the cow when he squeezed out
the milk, and the cats came around.
My fat cousin Robert who couldn't say Szostak
said Shoe Stack What's That and pissed

in the mud, pissing and pissing filling a hole.
He's Sleeping, they said, Your Grandpa is Sleeping.
He picked me up and gave me the reins.
Around and around the hayfield we rode.
Shouting Gee and Haw he patted my head.
He picked me up and gave me the reins.
In a wider and wider circle we rode.
I watched him climb in the apple tree.

Leave Him Be, Grandma said, Leave Him Be.
In late sunlight I followed him down to the creek.
In the late sunlight minnows skittered away.
Like little brown clouds they all moved away.
In the honeyed glow of a kerosene lamp on the table
he opened his book and we all moved away.
He lay his face on the water.
In the last light he entered the water.

PATRICIA GOEDICKE

One More Time

And next morning, at the medical center
Though the X-Ray Room swallows me whole,

Though cold crackles in the corridors
I brace myself against it and then relax.

Lying there on the polished steel table
Though I step right out of my body,

Suspended in icy silence
I look at myself from far off
Calmly, I feel free

Even though I'm not, now
Or ever:

The metal teeth of death bite
But spit me out

One more time:

When the technician says breathe
I breathe.

Coin of the Realm

So what if the underside of it's
not silver

no lining but cheap

nickels dimes quarters
in a change purse, the

flip side

of the coin we need to
protect ourselves, whatever

income tax we pay
for guns helps keep us in

schoolbooks

he said, tucking away the
popular rifle under the car seat

outside the playground

for emergency use
only

wouldn't you agree

in order to make an omelet
you have to break some eggs

for most experiments to succeed

the price of conquering disease
comes high

heads, tails

after the carnage the crack
dealers return like jackals

sniffing

the shells of several hundred
Chevrolets litter the beach

then there are the claws

my father the defense contractor
in order to put bacon on the table

my mother the big red
maw

one hand snaps at the other

in slippery pockets the
raw jingle of scratch

sometimes bleeds a little

unfortunately, he said
stepping all over his children's

lives and not even
noticing

first it's the left side of the brain
then it's the right

in the clockwise and counter clockwise
whirl of water

into a drinking glass, the clasp
and unclasp of atoms

the terrified heart listens
for the other half of its beat

he said, realistically
speaking

it is a sad fact

in a missile silo near Great Falls
Montana

it takes two men to count

without both of them nothing
would go off

JIM HALL

Reign of Terror

If they were pretty
or opened the door wide enough,
he would unlatch his raincoat and let
it spring out.
His eyes pleading
as if he were a beggar and this a withered hand.

Five said, "Jesus Christ!"
Most shrieked and bolted.
One laughed.
One cried.
And the last one invited him inside.

When the officers arrived
he mewled and denied it all.
They took him in.
The star witnesses assembled
but since no one had noticed his face`
they were all forced to study
five dangling suspects.

Still there was no positive identification.
Certainly nothing that could stand up in court.

The Reel World

Down from the tower, back at sea-level,
this is the shop where I work now,
with the ballyhoo, bait buckets, frozen squid,
the turquoise teasers, the rubbery worms
oiled for the slimy feel of authenticity.

Down here there is humility:
the twelve year old girl demanding
I pluck out the shrimp who'd lost its snap,
the drug dealer with his gobs of hundreds
buying golden reels, custom rods,
the cream of the shop,
the drunk who believed this was a grocery
and wouldn't be convinced.
No salami! No onion dip!

There is sympathy here as well:
the shrimp who glide in their tank
expecting the worst,
dreading the long trip back to the sea,
where they will be hooked just so,
so even they will begin to believe
they're free.

And best there is the art of duplication:
making myself seem to be a part of this,
here with the plugs, wooden replicas,
the mirror lures, the feathery jigs,
all proven fish-foolers. Here where I rig
dead mullet to invisible wire,
so to some hopeful creature below
it will appear lively and desirable.

The Figure a Poem Makes

A hundred is the most I ever made,
but mainly it's copies.
I ask you, what have you got
when what you've got no one will pay
you anything for except to print it up
and give three copies back to you?

O.K., so you take Jackie Kennedy and some sex
and you whip up 300 creamy

pages and get some New York fellow sweating
at his 1800 buck desk over it,
and you got yourself 5 big ones easy,
and if you got any luck lots where those
came from.

Frost was right. More than the truth
is about right.
But then he knew Jackie.
It helps to know Jackie.
Especially if you can get more out of it
than three lousy copies of what
you already got.

Maybe Dats Your Pwoblem Too

All my pwoblems
who knows, maybe evwybody's pwoblems
is due to da fact, due to da awful twuth
dat I am SPIDERMAN.

I know, I know. All da dumb jokes:
No flies on you, ha ha,
and da ones about what do I do wit all
doze extwa legs in bed. Well, dat's funny yeah.
But you twy being
SPIDERMAN for a month or two. Go ahead.

You get doze cwazy calls fwom da
Gubbener askin you to twap some booglar who's
only twying to wip off color T.V. sets.
Now, what do I cawre about T.V. sets?
But I pull on da suit, da stinkin suit,
wit da sucker cups on da fingers,
and get my wopes and wittle bundle of
equipment and den I go flying like cwazy
acwoss da town fwom woof top to woof top.

Till der he is. Some poor dumb color T.V. slob
and I fall on him and we westle a widdle
until I get him all woped. So big deal.

You tink when you SPIDERMAN
der's sometin big going to happen to you.
Well, I tell you what. It don't happen dat way.
Nuttin happens. Gubbener calls, I go.
Bwing him to powice, Gubbener calls again,
like dat over and over.

I tink I twy sometin diffunt. I tink I twy
sometin excitin like wacing cawrs. Sometin to make
my heart beat at a difwent wate.
But den you just can't quit being sometin like
SPIDERMAN.
You SPIDERMAN for life. Fowever. I can't even
buin my suit. It won't buin. It's fwame wesistent.
So maybe dat's youwr pwoblem too, who knows.
Maybe dat's da whole pwoblem wif evwytin.
Nobody can buin der suits, dey all fwame wesistent.
Who knows?

C. G. HANZLICEK

Room for Doubt

Two boys, using fish heads for bait,
Landed a four-foot angel shark.
Laid out on the pier,
It seemed never to take the right pose
For a serious study of it.
Again and again the boys moved it,

Poking fingers into its eye sockets
To drag it across the planks.

It was a creature worth studying:
Broad, blunt snout like a catfish,
White lips and belly
Under a black-speckled gray back,
And wide wings like a ray or a skate.
Dianne wanted to say many things,
But only looked out to sea
And asked how long sharks live in air.
Oh, a long time, the boys said.

I've heard all the stories
About the sluggish nerves of fish,
But if those stories are true,
Why did the shark tremble,
Pound the pier planks with its tail,
Each time forefingers sank
Knuckle-deep into its brow?

To Dianne and me the slaps and shudders
Looked a lot like pain.
What the hell, I don't care
If they were the crudest reflexes,
With no more feeling behind them
Than ripples rolling out on water
After a dropped stone.
What matters is the room for doubt,
The kind of room we all ask for.

In the Dark Again

Like a stone dropping down a well
The moon sets,
And once again I'm in the dark.
Oh, there's Vega and Rigel,
But the trees are black,

The crickets lost in the grass.
I've come this far
On two blind wings and no prayer,
But it feels natural,
It works,
And I'm not where I once was.
Forward is something,
Even if there are no high beams
To make the mile markers
Blaze along the road.
Besides, if it all had a single
Readable meaning,
Flashing like a blue beer sign,
I'd keep brushing it
Like a moth,
Lightly,
Without a thought in my head.

C. G. Hanzlicek
(after Atilla Jozsef)

Take my word for it, Hanzlicek,
I love you,
I can't help myself.
I live with a woman
Who wakes to your needs
And doesn't hate me for them.

We can compare life
To a worn shoe,
A car out of gas on a back road,
A lost ticket,
Yet in the end, beyond the metaphors,
We can't help loving life.

It would be nice
To buy a ticket to the self;

It must be somewhere inside.
We might arrive, though,
Too bored from the journey
To want to see the sights.

We might just lie on our backs
In the hotel room,
Counting brass spindles
On the footrail of the bed,
Having our meals sent up,
Dreaming another self.

JAMES HARMS

Breakfast on the Patio

Despite the weatherman, who in hibiscus
and a grass skirt waved this morning
at a map of clouds, Jeff pulls on a pair
of sunglasses to watch the people walk by.
What he really wants is to go sailing,
which is okay with me, but the harbor
is smooth as an oil slick and breathless.
We watch a parade of moms and carriages,
the babies cooing the sunshine,
and a line of cyclists all tanned to
oblivion. Jeff goes for more coffee,

the boy next door walks by wearing
chaps and plastic six shooters.
I wave at his mother who is hosing down
the walk, and she waves back. Then I say, Bang
to the little guy but he just looks at me.
So I say, Hi, and he just looks at me.
Jeff returns with another plate of toast.
He still wants to sail but I raise a wet finger

and he nods like, Maybe later, then shakes out
the newspaper. Another cyclist pedals by
going, I guess, 20 miles an hour; I watch
the hanging fuchsia stir a bit in the sudden
wind. The phone rings and I look over at Jeff
but he's reading so I think, Oh well, and get up
to answer it. At the door I stop because
Jeff has asked, "You know what?" and I'm waiting
for whatever what is. "It doesn't get much better,"
he says, and we laugh. Phone still ringing

I go inside; the tape clicks on across the room,
I hear myself telling someone I'm not home,
then I hear someone say, "You're never home,
the problem with you is you're never home."
It's Kay, who I decide to call back later
but she goes on. "The problem with you is
you're never home when you're home.
You're not there when I look at you.
You don't say a thing when you say something."
Kay is on a roll but I go over
and pick up the phone. I'm home, I say
and I hang up. Then I go outside and look
at the smooth water, so smooth it seems fake.
"Who was it?" Jeff asks, still reading the paper.
The Harbor Queen is chugging past, a crowd
of tourists waves at me from its deck.
I lift my hand and say, It was for you.

Explaining the Evening News to Corbyn
(after Ben Watt)

I heard Caruso last night for the first time, I'm 28.
My stepfather sat me in a lounge chair
the color of rain on new grass,
and said, "Listen, just listen." And I did.
Every time I express a fondness
he leaves an album out, a cassette tape by my car keys,

and with Caruso (like Rachmaninoff) it worked,
though I couldn't help saying the obvious,
how similar he seemed to Darby Crash.
One day you're eighteen in a freshman dorm,
gold and brown empties of Old English 800
crushed like metal cigarettes on the carpet—
The Lost Pilot is shaking in your hands.
Then it's Cavafy in a bathtub with
cinnamon candles welding themselves to the tiles
and the sprinklers outside interpreting rain.
Did I decide then never to have a child?

When I was sixteen I had never kissed a girl,
which is all you think about, aside from driving.
I would've nuzzled a broken bottle to hold Francesca's hand,
but what we said to each other
out of fear of saying anything
wasn't good for very much,
though it was better than whispering darkness
into a cup of clear water.
It wasn't true.
Corbyn lies in my arms now like the Prince of San Francisco.
His father, my oldest friend, laughs at me
from across the room because I can't keep
his baby's head from wobbling.
When I was Corbyn's age I had more hair
I think, and I might've been skinnier.
Kennedy was making plans
to bring Frost from Vermont
for the inauguration,
and life for my parents was as lyrical
as a cafeteria breakfast.
My sister will marry in a week
a man I've known and played tennis with
for twenty years. They sit with me now,
admiring Corbyn and thinking of names for a child
they are planning.
My sister has her hair tied back
like a Romanian gymnast, and when she looks at Corbyn

she smiles and is as beautiful as he is.
What I like about the evening news
is you can talk through it without missing anything,
which is what we're doing. But something's happened
            somewhere, so we
suddenly go quiet, as if an angel
in feathers has walked into the room.
I say, Corbyn, you're very lucky you can't hear any of this.
And then, like always, his head begins to wobble.
His mom reaches out to take him, and she kisses my cheek
in the same movement, so I feel relieved and scared
all at once, which is familiar enough to keep quiet about.
Corbyn's father walks toward the refrigerator
for a Coors and the dog puts his nose on my shoe.
It's a slow second and we wish
for a lot of things, the five of us,
for Corbyn to be okay forever
and for the child my sister hopes to have.
I suggest they call him Caruso, and we laugh.
What we really want, my sister says, is a little girl,
a little girl to marry Corbyn. Everyone's smiling.
An angel enters the room and it is clear:
we've got it all wrong.

My Androgynous Years

I had a crisis at the supermarket, yesterday.
I said to myself softly, so no one could hear,
I said, Your soul is *not* stepping
from your body. I said, Stop it, relax.
And I did. I held it all together
past the magazines and gum,
through 8-Items-or-Less and out the door.
I sat in my car and let mascara
run down my arms like greasy rain.
Until a woman in a Volvo beeped
and pointed at the asphalt under me,

unwilling, I guess, to wait any longer.
When I was eight my sister hated me.
She hated clothes and make-up.
She hated buckled shoes.
We'd walk Vermillion Street beneath
the insect sizzle of neon
to buy my mother cigarettes,
loiter like felons till
all seemed clear in Lee's Liquor-Mart.
I'd ask Peter Lee where the Cokes had gone
and he'd come around to help me look
while my sister snaked her hand to a packet
of Pall Malls and was gone. On the way home,
sometimes, she ran ahead, easy over long legs.
She'd find a crumbling vestibule
to soothe her shadow down to stone,
and time my slow arrival.
We'd sit near a puddle of ragwater
or piss, her laughter a hand against
my neck, and wait for my sobs to soften.
I share my lunch today with a boy from
Peru, Indiana. He recites King's
"I Have a Dream" speech
rising off the bench to shake his fists
at the assembled phantoms.
Pigeons scatter and regather, and all around us
haloes appear and vanish, the fountain mist
blown in rainbows and to pieces.
He is splendid and I offer all my Fritoes.
One night he will come to me like a dream
on the television, and announce
a special offer: laser-sharpened knives
or a three-record set.
But that's the future. For now
we hold hands and talk about the news,
which is much better than yesterday's
but only half as good as tomorrow's.

RICHARD HARTEIS

The Hermit's Curse

For a generation
he lived on the breast
of mountain, and the dry girls
would climb the hill
in search of health.

Always alone, wearing
their shame like a birthmark
the childless wives, themselves
often children, would stay three days
and nights. The hill was alive
with vipers and scorpions,
decaying bodies under shallow
rock piles: the holy man
lived in a stone-lined pit,
the center of the mountain cemetery.

The ghosts of desperate women
cool the rocks, stir the air.
Plastic amulets fly from a pole.
A holy man's trophies? Why these
scraps of sequined cloth,
rotting in the wind? For
the holy man has blown away.

The local mullah came
and prayed with him a week.
It took a week and more.
Then the helicopter came
and flew the holy man away.

A radar screen
scans the desert stars.
Gone the prophet's burning eyes,

the low fires, a young wife's
moaning.

In the valley once again some women
are childless. There is a government
study being made. They have
put superstition behind them.
They know about radiation.
They are demanding a wall to
protect them from the radar's
evil eye.

Mirage

In Memoriam,
Katharine Meredith Goldenberg

A stand of Queen Anne's Lace
catches the infrequent breeze—
a white sail lifting along the shore
where this year's growth of creatures
sends lazy bubbles to the stagnant surface.

A convoy of dragonflies swarms in,
hovers like a rainbow, and
disappears when a blue snake
glides across the lily pads
into the dark deep roots.

The country pond has reappeared, primeval,
as though the seasons never changed
and time stretched out into an infinity
of lime green light and midday heat.

But your memory sings out against that
illusion like a school bell calling for
the end of summer, like a silent angel
with flaming sword.

Was it only last year
you left the blazing heat
and burst into the cool stone cellar
to share a bucket of raspberries
you had picked at the pond's edge
when in your joy and change of light
missed a step and went all flying
staining the pretty sundress raspberry
gashing the smooth brown knees red
before I moved to help you.

How often did you stand like this in life:
vulnerable, a spoiled gift in hand, and
the dignity of a Pharoah.

I climb the granite steps
into the brilliant light
where you smile again
and the white sundress
glows against your tan shoulders.

The dark berries
are as cool and sweet
as forgiveness.

Genetics

for Audrey Garbisch

Yachts in the harbor
mirror the patterns
of geese in the sky
like an Escher painting.
The air has sharpened
and somewhere brown bears
are beginning to daydream.

Hardly in the autumn
of our lives, we cruise through

the pre-dawn fog camouflaging the
silver Mercedes and confess to each other
over steaming mugs of coffee how we've
come to relish the morning, our joy at
the beginning of the day as predictable
lately as lower back pain after lovemaking.

Are there beads on the double helix,
you wonder, which code for more than
the itch to reproduce yourself
or when to turn your hair grey?

What alarm is warning the heart
to love the light, forgive the darkness?
What coaches the blood to sing its praise
for the surprising gift as we reach the airport,
our farewell kiss a preparation and a covenant.

BROOKS HAXTON

Auspice

> first month dawn
>> with kindling at the back log
> small flames
>> shoots of winter wheat
> the smoke of honeylocust
>> on a sodden hillside

>> thunderheads upended over woods
>> soaked dark on the horizon

>> by swift passage of the solstice
> by doves paired
> even on barbed wire
>> at daybreak

by the keelbone and green shoulder
and blue neck flank
of the starling
dappled
in the daylong rivering of ten million
by the strut on earth of grackles
by good auspice in the bitter season

Jackie Andy
for the child born now
or soon or home already
for the warm indoors there
for safekeeping
of you three together

braided two-fold into the triple
outpour of these words

my love
that I braid you
and us
for one begotten now
of me and Francie
child of the long night

to be born us in September
under the sign of green persimmons
in the month of late sweet corn
and muscadines
and ripe melons
in the warm fall in the cooling season

when the one who has no thought of it this winter
sprawled on a blanket over the earth between you
under a splash of greenwood shade

shall creep and chortle
into the warm splashed sunlight
when the sumacs have caught wind of autumn

and time comes as now
          that what can be begins
              and keeps beginning

Traveling Company

Three blocks down, the leaves around the C&O Canal ignite
in a cloud of amber, salmon, rust, reflected where leaves fallen
float, with leaves turned parchment sunken into the reflections.

You'd like it here. Canvasback and widgeon, bufflehead, coot,
goose, and mallard on the reservoir midway in their migration,
hundreds of them, on near-freezing water, sleep.

The palette's earthier, but the glow builds in the morning
like Monet, at eighty-five, near blind, remembering
the water lilies in the paint he could not see.

Traffic passes, and the gold whorl of a winded elm unravels.
With huge canvas, with a memory of painting
on the raft at dawn, blind Monet,

pain in the arthritic knuckles
too familiar still to be distracting, worked
the aches and stabs of color melting

into the world's transfiguration
strokes of upright poplar trunks thrust
into the mirror underwater

obscure slope of river bottom smudged
with small clouds drifting in flotilla
lily pads mapped on the river's surface

on the canvas— planes inextricable in release
transparent fused
green waters blue cloudcolor mud

under the pupil mixed in
dying into the living
into the traveling company of that vision.

Jean, you've given us your books of poems, full,
and deep, and fused, and clear,
and this book, our engagement present, empty.

Francie lets me use her half of every page,
whichever half that is, a gift like yours, and like Monet's,
requiring thought to fill it.

Meanwhile the elm leaves drop, and canvasbacks, complaining
in an ancient tongue, with bray of sinew and hoarfrosted wing,
have burst from the water over the southern skyline.

ANN HAYES

Pietá

This figure mourns that figure hanging dead,
Each marble face an emblem, sacrifice
Born of its pity, fury seen with love.
The hammer fell upon a lifted arm,
Fell on a face, smashed at an eye, a nose.
What did he want, what did he think to kill,
What urgent holiness did he believe
Who called himself the Christ and struck at stone?

Send flowers to the altar, holy place.
New to the shock we come, we gasp and sigh,
Mourning for surface lost, for stone and light,
Waste of a passion borne and spent, of skill

That cut as surgeons cut to quicken life.
What fury held a hand as firm as stone?
What fury turned the marble into flesh?
The living and the dead, who gave us both?

The Holy Father is householder here
And is instinct to pray. O pray for us,
You who believe in prayer, to find a place
Where life embodied in the arms of love
Can mourn its dead. Madonna made of stone,
Powder of marble, dust upon the air,
We saw your face that others will not see.
Lady of griefs, what image do you keep?

Much Ado About Nothing, Thanksgiving, 1972

They have a few amusements, presidents,
Drop into restaurants they used to like
After the secret service clears the way;
Simpler, I guess, to stay at home with friends,
Open the bourbon there and talk and laugh;
And yet sometimes a public man can wish
To have the pleasant time the public has.
The Nixons took a moment of success
After election, easy mandate in,
After Thanksgiving with the country safe.
Public and private, New York theater,
They made a party: men in business suits,
His wife beside him, Bebe, both the girls,
All shining, smiling, waving, shirted, furred;
And other men who kept their backs to him
Sat nearby on the aisles and looked at us.
The play was a success but nothing nude
And nothing controversial: current hit,
Shakespeare revived and made American.

The plot of *Much Ado*? Old foolishness,
Old tales again: young men returned from war

Into a merry war, to laughing trials
Of wit upon each other, brothers' quarrels,
A hidden search for love: though much ado,
Nothing it is, a smiling social world
Where everyone observes and masquerades
And some who speak the truth have wounding tongues.
Remember nothing? Semblances and lies
Are false belief and action spied upon,
Accomplished plots deliberately played.
You do remember innocence ashamed,
Shallow though it may be, yet lost, disgraced,
Begrimed by a pretense. But there's the Watch
Who catch the villains though they cannot tell
Flat burglary from slander, muddle all
Until frustration tells the truth of crime:
Eavesdropping, lies, deception and pretense,
A comedy before our president.

I watched him watch. I was across the aisle
A row away, with murder in my heart
Though he was safe with me, needed no men
To stand between his beating heart and mine.
I would not touch him. But I shook with hate
And horror at my hatred, not so felt
Until I stood so near: the bitter years,
How they had prospered him! I told the names
For slandered lives behind him. Did they hate?
Surely they tasted acid I could taste.
How well he played on fear, how well he knew
What we would shudder from, what we'd protect.
Meanwhile the play was playing: Benedick
Swore that he'd been defamed by Lady Tongue,
The audience saw through and laughed him down.
Did Warren hate him? In that old campaign
When votes were traded and the big chance came,
What was a promise? Warren understood,
That I believe, and left him to contempt.

We who can see the cast and feel the spell
Continuously unwinding, shall we know

The justice from the thief? I watched and he,
Gazed at the constables who brought the law,
Gazed at a show of penitence and grief.
Now can we tell deception, now be sure
Which friend to trust, which bride to bring to bed?
There was applause and laughter, there was love
Successfully recovered, partners found
And all put right within a little world
Where old, old instances remain to mock
But wit can still be true. We turned to him,
Turned from the bowing stage to see his bow,
And some applauded loud but others hissed,
Others like me, even in that success,
We hissed and cried at him. He took our cries,
He smiled and waved, he made the outrage last.
World of good neighbours lost, I heard my voice,
Liar, it cried, liar, you lie, you lie.

JUDY PAGE HEITZMAN

Spaces

When you lay sick that spring, too weak to move
on the mattress that floated like a dock at the end of a pier,
I stopped going to my classes, kept straining my eyes
to count the moles on your chest.
It was better than sex the way you lay awake,
letting me sleep.

The next winter on Skyline Drive we both felt a need to enter,
to make a place as open as plowed earth
that folds back, keeps folding back into itself.
I thought I was safe, longed for a house.
What did it matter to us
that years lay like snow across a field?

There was even a kind of lust when, after you spent your love
at her white breasts, you came back to our hot room.
Can we try again? you whispered, and I said *yes* though I knew,
as you did, that it was only that it felt good,
that no matter how many times we changed the sheets
we would still sweat.

I have stopped counting seasons. This morning the dream
I was dreaming ended.
I know how it feels to thirst,
to be so tired I would kill to get some sleep.
Once I wanted a baby.
The way I feel now is nothing like that.

March

Jerome Lallier said to ride in his sleigh
when he collected sap from the maple trees.
We began in his woods
where all the pails were protected by little
peaked roofs over the spouts. It felt dangerous
in our woods, the stream to cross, me not sure
where his property became ours. I don't think
my father ever said he could tap our trees,
but he did it anyway, the same way he watered down his milk.
I have never seen harvests like this since, unless
it is apples. Those in our back yard are not cared
for, we don't spray, and the ones that fall
ferment and squish under our feet when we mow
the lawn. I love them in buckets,
and the smaller baskets with curved handles.
There is never the after-harvest, only the sense of plenty.
Sometimes I think I should ride my bicycle
and see the whole thing.
When the sky darkened
I'd go into the house, turn the lights on,
leave the door open, and listen for the wind.

Jonathan Holden

Losers

*"The best part of NFL playoff games
is those shots of the losing bench."*

— *overheard in a bar*

Without their helmets,
their faces betray everything:
defeat, an open political
scandal. Some are
crying. I want to thank
them: They admit. I'd like to shake
their homely, trustworthy hands.
But they just sit there,
each of them going
over his own private score
again, checking the bland words
of his rejection

like a man sorting slowly
through all of the flattering
hackneyed constructions
his lover had once placed
on his eyes, on his mere
hands—*I'll do anything
for you*—each word a smooth
flat stone, a *tabula
rasa* he still strokes absently
under his thumb, remembering
when the act of simply
unbuckling his belt
was cruel,
a command that could crush
her parts of speech to a single
vowel, the same
stark question begging

his answer—a short
hard retort he'd thought only he
could give her again
and again—what he'd always
suspected of his true
worth, the secret he'd scarcely dared
whisper even to her—

Not like these
men, slumped on the losing
bench, staring ahead, trying
to comprehend the rudiments
of some old standard system of
weights and measures
they'd once learned they had
to go by—
these men who, out of
power now, relieved
of their secrets, are as honestly
miserable as they look.

Falling from Stardom
for S.

When only the human remains,
our two human faces licked clean
of disguises like two friends,
I understand what an ex-lover meant
when she said she was tired
of fucking celebrities,
how this star director
who confessed he'd grown bored
with practicing stunts
on one trapeze at a time
turned out in the end to be
no more than his assortment of methods.
The persuasion in his hands,
even the tropical weather moving

through his melancholy eyes,
seemed to her ulterior.
On the mattress with him
she was a mirror.

I have friends who are afraid
to say something trite.
Every rejoinder must top what was just said.
Their gossip's hilarious,
it's a compost of envies. They'll tell you
the sex habits of each president.
At 50, they would still live as we did
before we gave up counting
the nervous thrills in this world
and bore our children.
But their mouths are chameleon, their faces
want definition, are composites of all
our faces, and we
are the score which they cannot stop keeping.
When they lend us themselves
they use the word *love*.
They would finish with us
as with a piece of heavy equipment.
Their motion's a form of immunity.
Loneliness gives them freedom to move.

I wake with you, now, and for the first time
that I can remember
I envy nothing.
The morning's singular,
it will not refer.
Am I naïve?
Is this some child's drawing?
There's a blue brook. On it, a boat.
One cloud. One bird. The sun
faithful, always righthanded,
scatters its sticks of lemony candy.
Everything's loyal.
The boat wants only to be a boat,

the cloud a cloud,
the bird bird,
the brook. If the word *love* means anything
it must be like this—
how two sticks of sun that fall in the brook
can shine all morning, shine
beneath fame, the water descending
without demur, filling
one place at a time.

Liberace

It took generations to mature
this figure. Every day it
had to be caught sneaking off
to its piano lesson and beaten up.
Every day it came back
for more. It would have been
trampled underground, but
like a drop of mercury, it was
too slippery. Stamped on,
it would divide, squirt away
and gather somewhere else, it was
insoluble, it had nowhere to go.
All it could do was gather again,
a puddle in the desert, festering
until the water had gone punk, it
was no good for anything anymore.
It wears rubies on its fingers now.
Between its dimples, its leer is
fixed. Its cheeks are
chocked, its eyes twinkle. It
knows. Thank you, it breathes
with ointment in its voice,
Thank you very much.

COLLETTE INEZ

The Woman Who Loved Worms
(from a Japanese Legend)

Disdaining butterflies
as frivolous,
she puttered with caterpillars,
and wore a coarse kimono,
crinkled and loose at the neck.

Refused to tweeze her brows
to crescents,
and scowled beneath dark bands
of caterpillar fur.

Even the stationery
on which she scrawled
unkempt calligraphy,
startled the jade-inlaid
indolent ladies,
whom she despised
like the butterflies
wafting kimono sleeves
through senseless poems
about moonsets and peonies;
popular rot of the times.

No, she loved worms,
blackening the moon of her nails
with mud and slugs,
root gnawing grubs,
and the wing case of beetles.

And crouched in the garden,
tugging at her unpinned hair,
weevils queuing across her bare
and unbound feet.

Swift as wasps, the years.
Midge, tick and maggot words
crowded her haikus
and lines on her skin turned her old,
thin as a spinster cricket.

Noon in the snow pavilion,
gulping heated saki
she recalled Lord Unamuro,
preposterous toad
squatting by the teatray,
proposing with conditions
a suitable marriage.

Ha! She stoned imaginary butterflies,
and pinching dirt,
crawled to death's cocoon
dragging a moth to inspect
in the long afternoon.

The Old Lady Across the Hall
Has Gone to Live Behind the Door

In a country of drifting spectacles
she flicks on the hours and dials the sun.
The track of time moves gray on gray;
her mind daubs in the colors,
converts a blurred announcer's eyes
to mauve chiffon, her aureole
when old beaux drove the Landaus down
macadam roads to home.
The screen explodes its Catherine Wheels
and spins her into yawning.
Transfixed, she twirls the starbox off.
Herself alone behind a door,
twiddling years on yellow thumbs
before a blur of furniture.

Slumnight

T.V. gunning down
the hours
serves as sheriff
in a room
where one yawn
triggers off another,

sends time scuffling
into night.
Wars slugged out
on vacant lots
sign an armistice
with sleep.

Turned to a wall,
the children dream
and the moon pulls up
in a squadcar.

Instructions for the Erection
of a Statue to Myself in Central Park

Let me be formed with stone;
a slab of diorite between my ears
will do for brains,
a round cut ruby for a heart.

Breasts? Alabaster mounds
that will not sag from suckling time,
against which birds will bat their wings
and rain will stroke and wind . . .

Cold to sex, and blood, and birth,
drape my marble thighs with snow.
Then let the lovers, hot with quarreling and tears,
stand in my shadow and kiss.

DAVID JAMES

Harvest

The combine grinds into the hearts
of pheasants and quail as it mows
through the wheat field,
a knife slicing off wedges
row by row.
A distant hawk
glides in a sky
too clear to believe.
Harvest settles in the fields
and homes, in the slow heads
of cattle, the excited breath
of a young girl running
around the side of the barn.

Smoking and sounding for miles,
the combine turns back the other way.
A cloud of mashed wheat
spirals behind it,
fading into air.
In an open grass field,
cows graze around
two boys who are crawling,
giggling, trying to moo
their way into the herd.

And behind the whole length of day,
the pulse of the combine
is steady and sure.
From as far as the Jeddo cemetery
where trees empty
and leaves soak down into graves,
you can see grain smoke
rising over the combine,

dozens of seagulls touching
down in the cut row,
until another orange moon
stands up to the dusk
and wins.

The Love of Water Faucets

*"In captivity, they often develop an inordinate love
of water faucets and will lie under them for hours."*

— *Ring Tailed Lemurs, Calgary Zoo*

It's no more peculiar
than dyeing your hair orange
or eating head cheese.
You know & I know
we do stranger things
with miscellaneous fixtures.
So they get turned on
by water faucets. So what?
Maybe it's the smooth curve,
the easy down spout nature
of the pipes. Or the color,
the shine and reflection,
or the ring free tail-like look.
They envision the rest of an animal
embedded in the wall, the cement,
begging for sympathy.
Or perhaps they lie under water faucets
for hours, staring up into that dark,
circle mouth, the size of a lemur's, wide open,
to imagine a blackness,
a scene in the deepest rain forest,
where they dream of being
afraid and running and
alive.

The Blind Man Who Sells Brushes

A blind man selling brushes
walks across the lawn, up the
front steps and knocks on your
door. From behind the living
room curtains you stare at his
white eyes rolling backwards
against his brain. The moment
you saw him coming, you sent
the kids to the basement, shut
the windows, turned the radio off,
locked the front door. You figured
the blind man would just move on to
your neighbor's house. He drops his
black suitcase on the porch and
begins pounding on your screen.

The house is perfectly quiet.
Near dinnertime you bring the children
upstairs. Your husband parks
the car down the street
and sneaks through the neighbor's
yard to the back door. The blind
man is smashing the screen with
his cane. The huge suitcase stuffed
with brushes falls off the porch
into the rose garden.

After dinner the family tiptoes
downstairs to watch TV without
the sound. Your husband taps his foot
to the beating of the blind man who
wants to sell brushes to you.
When it is time, you silently
put the children to bed.
The blind man is swinging at the door knob
with his cane. Your husband climbs under

the covers. You lean over, pull your knees up,
breathing into his back.

In the morning the blind man's head
is screaming through the storm window.
You and the kids sit at the breakfast table,
heads bowed, praying:
O God, *please let us kill him.*

Mark Jarman

Cavafy in Redondo

Our ruins run back to memory.
Stucco palaces, pleasure bungalows, the honeycomb
of the beachcombers' cluster of rentals—
I remember them, filings in sand
pricking up at the magnet of nostalgia,
a sigh of dusty filaments. Our ruins
wear the as-yet-unruined like coral crowns.
Night life blows through the boardwalk's
conch-shell coils of neon, skirting the water.
This was never—ask my parents—a great city.
It had its charm, like a clear tidal shallows,
silted-in now, poldered, substantial, solid,
set for the jellying quake everyone expects.

I walked these streets one night with a new lover,
an as-yet-to-be lover— it took a whole night
of persuasion. I had been gone a year,
and walked as sea mist compounded the dew.
My legs ached by the time bed was agreed to.
How sentimental it was, to flatter, listen,
cajole, make little whining endearments,
plodding ritualistically among landmarks,
sandy shrines in alleys, the black meccas
of plate-glass windows fronting the beach

where white froth reflected in the night.
I kept that ache, not love's, after we parted.

We did not part to history with its glosses;
we were not even footnotes. Our ruins
will bear out no epics or histories here,
footprints compounded of dew and fog
and under them, maybe a rusty antique
that, boiled in acids, will tell a tale.
After all, ships passed, broke up on the point.
Mainly, the beach eroded in great ridges
until ground cover belted it back. A pleasure dome
was dismantled, certain fashions
of dress and of love. History builds to last,
crumbles to last, shakes off its dust
under the delicate excavating brush— to last.

Built above the beach was a colossus,
humped and strutted and roaring with many voices.
Winds chased through it screeching and then
it stood silent. People flocked to it, entered it,
and though not lost, screamed as if tortured.
I am joking. There was a roller coaster
of some note and no small size. Where did it go?
Ah, yes, lost in the coral make-up
of that teetering lover who walked beside me,
tired of my harangue, the persuasive underlove
that wanted to rise to the lips, those lips
colored by fuming street lamps.

Young, my parents drove out from a distant city,
through tawny hills medallioned with oak.
I have seen their worn postcards of the town,
a tide pool of neighborhoods mantled around
by semi-wilderness and orange groves.
Missiles came to squat above our house
on a benchmarked hill, turned obsolete,
and floated away on flatbeds, ruptured patios in their places.
We, too, left that house that heard,
in every lath and windowpane, the industry of phosphorus,

grinding out the waves in the late darkness.
My parents—all of us—have come and gone and left
no ghosts here, and that is our good fortune,
to give it all to the ocean, the troubled sleeper.

The Mirror

Outside is the untreed, tearless light,
palest and hardest when it falls,
as it falls here, on white stucco
on a hill of tar-banded concrete.
If I open the door, she tells me,
the light will make our work harder.

It is morning but the blinds protect
the softness of a late afternoon.
Every mirror in the house
is masked in a flesh-colored paste.
As we rub the wide sheet above the sofa
our faces appear in moon rilles and seas.

Grandmother and child, almost anonymous,
in that light and those fragments.
Gilbert Olivas knocks, Brad Arquette
scratches the screen door. Their voices,
calling me, hang in the dimness.
I don't open the door. I don't answer.

I don't know why every morning
we must clean the mirrors and keep out
the sun. But I love this spell,
tired, watching her arm muscle tense,
thin as a slat, hearing the glass
moan, Brad and Gilbert long gone.

She wears the set look she will die with
but I don't know that. I'll be told
to remember it, that frown of intention,

and a few words she said for me,
years from now, my mother fixing my tie
in the front hall, turning me toward the mirror.

The Supremes

In Ball's Market after surfing till noon,
we stand in wet trunks, shivering
as icing dissolves off our sweet rolls
inside the heat-blued counter oven,
when they appear on his portable TV,
riding a float of chiffon as frothy
as the peeling curl of a wave.
The parade M.C. talks up their hits
and their new houses outside of Detroit
and old Ball clicks his tongue.
Gloved up to their elbows, their hands raised
toward us palm out, they sing,
"Stop! In the Name of Love" and don't stop
but slip into the lower foreground.

Every day of a summer can turn,
from one moment, into a single day.
I saw Diana Ross in her first film
play a brief scene by the Pacific—
and that was the summer it brought back.
Mornings we paddled out, the waves
would be little more than embellishments:
lathework and spun glass,
gray-green with cold, but flawless.
When the sun burned through the light fog,
they would warm and swell,
wind-scaled and ragged,
and radios up and down the beach
would burst on with her voice.

She must remember that summer
somewhat differently, and so must the two
who sang with her in long matching gowns,

standing a step back on her left and right,
as the camera tracked them
into our eyes in Ball's Market.
But what could we know, tanned white boys,
wiping sugar and salt from our mouths
and leaning forward to feel their song?
Not much, except to feel it
ravel us up like a wave
in the silk of white water,
simply, sweetly, repeatedly,
and just as quickly let go.

We didn't stop either, which is how
we vanished, too, parting like spray—
Ball's Market, my friends and I.
Dredgers ruined the waves,
those continuous dawn perfections,
and Ball sold high to the high rises
cresting over them. His flight out of L.A.,
heading for Vegas, would have banked
above the wavering lines of surf.
He may have seen them. I have,
leaving again for points north and east,
glancing down as the plane turns.
From that height they still look frail and frozen,
full of simple sweetness and repetition.

DAVID KELLER

Mussels

Each time it's a surprise, finding a shell
on the beach, each one different;
like a childhood, the one that sought you out
without your knowing. How natural it feels
to the hand. I always think

they're white, but this one's dark.
Inside it is a tea-stained tongue,
the soft sound of inlets to the sea
at the tide's running, shallow ripples
and the reflections over the shells like gold,
a man spreading his good fortune
from a leather pouch onto the scale pan,
weighing in the gold to send money home.

In the kitchen are dozens of mussels
with the dirt and rough manners scrubbed off.
We will have them cooked in white wine.
It is impossible, there are so many.
How large the ocean must be,
and the man from the strict plains states
who first came on a hill, an Indian mound
of shells, amazed at these discarded moons,
thousands, an entire history of desire.
After the last one is gone
we will swab our plates with French bread
and sop up the fragrant yellow sauce,
rich and silent in the imagining as gold.

In the Middle of the Journey

I recognized her and stopped to say I owned
two of her prints. She'd moved, leaving
her husband, she said, and asked what I did
and wanted me to send her some of my poems
which pleased me and felt embarrassing, and said,
Don't be one of those people who never write
after they promise to. Every so often
I am reminded of her face, its kindness.
My wife left me. Everything's difficult.
I have a new wife. Soon there will be time
to put up the prints in this house; but it's true,
I am less good a man than I'd thought, and I
am sorry you know it, Sandra, I have lied
to women. I thought I had to.

Friends, Outside, Night

They are probably married or gone by now,
the two children Ralph had,
beginning that summer.
He'd rented a whole house;
that was what seemed strange at first.

One failing light reached part-way
upstairs toward the bedrooms.
The worst nights we sat on the porch,
passing along the hallway
to the old kitchen for more ice,

a neighborhood where no one familiar lived.
This is a serious matter,
an entire house said, windows
wide open to catch any stray eddy.
Even that late it stayed hot

and upstairs the children were sleeping,
arrived a few days before from his ex-wife.
I still think I can hear
their breathing, the dark dreams.
Hours after I should have been home

we sat and talked, laughing,
studying that occupation of older men,
or walked the dark hall to the kitchen
—the way I talk to people now—holding
the place against further loss.

MARY KINZIE

Xenophilia

Out in the northeast banks of thunderous
surly steel and white clouds bustle past.
The sky's en route this rugged March and edged
with mauve. In the midwest these are as near
as one can get to Alp crevasse or butte
these densely bottomed white tipped banks of cloud.
(Heather's in the foothills and juniper thrives
dusty with blue berries right up to the fall line.)

Terrarium ferns exude and arch their tender
selves in a glass box on the sill. Perhaps
the scudding heaven amuses and excites
great drops of moisture from their tropic lungs.
Still they seem to flutter caged to soar
and sympathize with nature's cousinage
the clouds and blackened bracts of trees that catch
flail and shudder in the tow of the sky.

We're in that early land of hand on hand and eye
to misty eye of endless cash and silver
pitchers full of cream and small cigars
and agate rings and sweeping luncheon points
achieved with tan expansive flourishings
amid the tremors of cyclamen and petals
glued to the running secret will of swimming
pools that slide in an absurd sweet compass;

or in that land of kirsch gâteaux and rich
cadeaux that do not fit and one won't wear
but once and taken off roll finally
into the woolly corner of a five star
muffled afternoon of love and drapery
when sex is hard to tell from tastes of foods

and velvety epergnes and satiny satis
factions or from marble beasts on boulevards;

or in that land of early rising lucid
tarn and buttery daffodil where higher
up by cable train the junipers
really stop and one slants on to upper
realms of ice and peak and tinkling sky
whose blue is a religious and sinister
idea and eyes are emblems out of hell
and rock and leap and sun pour slyly by;

or in *this* land which is like all the others now
that love is something over lived in once
done savored suffered through in ultimate
desire so rare and sterile from fidelity
from nearness craving to be much more near
that hyperventilation makes each breath
the next to dying in the creamy sunny air and
bodies fill with scarp and sheer descent;

in this land which is the mute midwest
postscripted to some golden lost epistle
we can no longer rest with being late born
and subdued to what we've loved and cost
bought outright or incurred among the mountains
by our absolutes. The debits will not
go and love will stay forever so
wrenching frightening and unfamiliar.

Indefinite indebtedness of feeling
whirring beneath us like the massive prop
that violets broad waters where they stretch
in sun or wrinkle under rain or frothing
across blue thigh and breast will make us rise
leaping and electric when rags of fog
sweep down us and globes of brain and organ lurch
with passing salts and distances and hopes.

Impromptu

In the frontroom I dance
because of dreaming summer
and the shape years do not yet have,

because screens let the inner out
and guard, from moths,
a gentle penetration for my lights
into evening, and the guarded evening plot.

Between myrtle, there,
a sharp wax holly hedge,
and the applause of locusts,
Grandfather silvers.

I hope to catch, by glimpses
he would catch of me
in yards of printed arabesque,

some locking center
of affection for him
which never kept its place—

which swivelled
till he died

and spun ankledeep,
and vain

    my wrists O
    lovely lovelier

across the ballet-sweetening
streamers in his eyes.

Elizabeth Kirschner

Two Blue Swans

My mother and father are two wounds, hanging
like ear lobes. Each day I pierce them

with jewels: rubies, pearls, tempered bits
of gold. Or think of them as shriveled ovaries

between which I, a blossom of being,
float. My beauty is their manifest.

I am the chance they never had.
Snow monkeys have been known, when their offspring

are stillborn, to carry the corpse with them
for days, even weeks. They nurture the dead.

I clutch the shrunken heads
of my mother and father. Tear them from me

and I will shriek, madly. In my dreams,
two blue swans unfurl magnificently and mate,

and rise. I roll toward my lover in the bed. And so
the moon and snowy rain press

upon my windows. And so my mother and father
tumble like an afterbirth. I let them out

like fabric, like stitches from my flesh.
And so, I am the afterlife, the glow

they felt when young and in love.
When nearing for that first great kiss.

The Blueness of Stars

The stars, the implacable stars
stay where they are
because it is
so— one design
worn to dust
like the rug in the foyer
of my childhood home.

That foyer was cold as a well.
Around the rug, slate formed
a night sky whose circumference
I danced more like a fairy
than an ordinary child.

Each slab of slate was a turtle's back,
a looking glass or palace marble.
Most definitely, a shifting scene,
the escalator that goes up and up . . .

I could have risen then, bodiless,
dusty as yeast, for I knew bits
of magic, ballet leaps,
levitations

learned at slumber parties.
Anything would have lifted me,

but each morning my legs pumped
under the chair at the breakfast table

as if I were on a swing.
The cinnamon toast I crunched on
were my own wings dusted with desire.

My mother's hair, even then, the color of ash
painted on my forehead at the beginning of Lent.
I wanted to die for her
whenever I stared at that back

bent at the stove on school day mornings
and probably did
as I suffered my way in adulthood.

I loved any man who resembled her
particular cache of shadow—
those whose words were sick
with self-hate, whose bodies
were boards, whose organs
were swimming in drink.

I loved each one singly,
wholly, under the blueness of stars,
forgetting once again,
I was an ordinary
woman who longed,
rightfully, for ordinary love—

my body the fantasy
I could have risen from.

I am my mother's daughter,
after all. Rigid

in conception, stuck as stars.
And although I still love
to make up for the losses,
I've shed her sickness
through the rigors of grief.
Yet, even in daytime
when the sun burns
the wick of that child stuck down deep,
the blueness of stars can
cast its dreamy haze and I begin
to move about again in slow
deliberate circles, numb
as a thumb, this strange
inward, flighty
thing.

The Fall of Light

I believe if I look over my shoulder,
there will be sunlight. I fall for this illusion
every minute or so. It is tedious
and tricky as love. What is not in us,
we want about us. Children. The fall
of light. Love. Once I was small enough
to fit inside my father's pocket. He fed me
orange seeds. I talked to him as though
he were a doll. "Now it's time for bed."
"Now it's time to rise." Obedient father,
what happened to us? How come I grew
to the size of a woman while my love,
small as a marble, rolled oggle-eyed
into the darkness? When I look over my shoulder,
I see mist. Black branches poke out
like the arms of someone deceased.
Up and around, there are birds. I follow
the birds. Their flight, upsweeping
toward light, toward air.

TED KOOSER

The Gilbert Stuart Portrait of Washington

You know it as well as the back of your hand,
that face like a blushing bouquet
of pink peonies set in the shadows of war,
the father of our country, patient,
sucking the past from his wooden teeth.

His famous portrait, never completed,
hung on the wall, at the front of the classroom
next to a black octagonal clock

137

with the ghost of a teacher trapped inside,
tapping out time with a piece of chalk.

It was easy to see his attention
was elsewhere. He'd left a dozen campfires
burning out there at the front of his face,
then retreated behind them. At fifty-eight,
he was old and broken. This was no way

to use up the days of a soldier.
Celebrity irked him. He had little time
for the likes of Gilbert Stuart, that son
of a snuff-grinding Tory, that slackard
who sat out the war with the English.

Perched on a chair in a cold stone barn,
according to Stuart, he smiled only once,
when a stallion ran past. He cared more
for thoroughbred horses and farming
than he did for the presidency.

On the wall between us and the future,
at the point where all of the lines converged,
George Washington, like any other man,
suppressed a deep sigh. So heavy was life;
how futile it seemed to protest.

We learned our lessons while the big clock
clacked, its Roman numerals arranged
in a wreath and sealed under glass. Those were
lovely calico autumns; then winter passed
with its long, clean pennants of light;

then spring with its chaffy rustle. We thought
those aisles were parallel, that our days
would never arrive at the vanishing point.
Before us always, he who could never tell a lie
kept his jaws closed on the truth.

A Finding

One of my dogs has brought the foreleg of a deer
up from the bottom woods, and gnawed on it a while,
and left it next to the door like a long-stemmed rose,
the joint at its shoulder red and flowering
where the dog has nearly licked the earth away.

Often they die like that, gut-shot by a hunter
or carrying an arrow for miles. I've found their bones
up under banks where they've hidden in caves of roots,
curled themselves over their pain, and kicked at the coyotes.
And the dogs have found far more of them than I.

Picking it up, a delicate life runs lightly
over my hands. The knee-joint's smooth articulation
folds the leg into itself like a carpenter's rule.
There's a spring to these bones, the hair laid back from flying,
the hoof like a castanet ready to clatter.

The wind lifts just a little, gets in under the fur,
and I see on the shin a tiny, tar-black scar
from a barbed-wire fence leapt not so long ago.
My two dogs stand and look over the fields,
and the three of us can hear that wire still thrumming.

The Afterlife

It will be February there,
a foreign-language newspaper
rolling along the dock
in an icy wind, a few
old winos wiping their eyes
over a barrel of fire;
down the new streets, mad women
shaking rats from their mops
on each stoop, and odd,
twisted children,

playing with matches and knives.
Then, behind us, trombones:
the horns of the tugs
turning our great gray ship
back into the mist.

LARRY LEVIS

For Zbigniew Herbert, Summer, 1971, Los Angeles

No matter how hard I listen, the wind speaks
One syllable, which has no comfort in it—
Only a rasping of air through the dead elm.
*
Once a poet told me of his friend who was torn apart
By two pigs in a field in Poland. The man
Was a prisoner of the Nazis, and they watched,
He said, with interest and drunken approval . . .
If terror is a state of complete understanding,

Then there was probably a point at which the man
Went mad, and felt nothing, though certainly
He understood everything that was there: after all,
He could see blood splash beneath him on the stubble,
He could hear singing float toward him from the barracks.
*
And though I don't know much about madness,
I know it lives in the thin body like a harp
Behind the rib cage. It makes it painful to move.
And when you kneel in madness your knees are glass,
And so you must stand up again with great care.
*
Maybe this wind was what he heard in 1941.
Maybe I have raised a dead man into this air,
And now I will have to bury him inside my body,
And breathe him in, and do nothing but listen—

Until I hear the black blood rushing over
The stone of my skull, and believe it is music.

But some things are not possible on the earth.
And that is why people make poems about the dead.
And the dead watch over them, until they are finished:
Until their hands feel like glass on the page,
And snow collects in the blind eyes of statues.

Magnolia

If I knew a way, I would tell you.
The man who threw a bottle from a passing car
At a young couple on a porch simply
Disappears into the night.

Still, I have my reasons for coming back
To this town, to these
Bright initials carved into an oak tree.
It is in leaf, and just now
It is shading a bare place in the park where
Two lovers are lying. Sunlight
And shadow dapple the woman's skirt
While she tries to figure out something with a stick—
Tracing the problem on the gray earth until
All of the lines intersect like a web, or a nest.
The man beside her is pretending to be asleep.
He looks pale and naïve with his eyes closed.
He looks as if he is remembering being young,
And an addict, because he is.
At 19, how it made the sun of damp places
Darken a little.
But not enough.
It was never enough,
And there was always this waiting for someone
To show up.
But before the singing began in his veins,
And engraved them again,
There were even a few pure moments,

More honest than clouds, or sunlight, or any
Blossoming thing beside him,
While he waited, and while he remembered
The hand of a friend growing cold in his hand—
How they were just watching
A concert together, and how
His friend died like that, casually,
As if he had decided not to listen anymore.
He left him lying there on the grass in Golden Gate Park,
And walked for an hour through Flieschacker Zoo.

I suppose he likes this oak tree, now, because
It doesn't judge him, and because it seems only
Amazed to be here, in leaf, and still standing.
I won't judge him, either.
Caught always in the spring of my 33rd year,
I hope I will not have to judge anyone
Singular and hopeless in the salt of his dying.
If I knew a way, I would tell him.
Though I would not tell him
That I died listening
To my own blood sing in the unheard registers
Of ice, and flowers— and lost it, finally,
In the most difficult passage.
If I knew a way, I would come up
The long, graying grass of this hill, and tell him,
And hold the thin shoulders of this man and this
Woman, who are ashamed, by now,
To *have* shoulders,
And tell them that it doesn't matter, that feeling
Your skin grow cold, and sudden,
Doesn't matter.

I would lie to them both, even now.
Because in the end, it was humiliating.
In the end, I was simplified, like a wild,
White Magnolia blossom I once saw. It was turning
Slowly brown in the hand of a schoolboy
While he kept staring patiently out
The rain streaked windows of a bus.

The Cocoon

Must have dreamed itself.

A small, gray hammock of unconcern,
It is not the witness of anything.

It waits, when it has finished,
Among hundreds just like it,

Hung in midair, in a privacy
Nothing disturbs.   This one,

So smug with its plan,
Still keeps the moisture

Of death in its fat.   It glistens,
And a thrill runs through it:

The burned, perfect face is emerging,
The serious little torso.   And this light,

This annihilation on each wing,
Seems to be singing its anthem.

It wobbles, then grows steady,
As the eyes that see nothing special

Stare at a last patch of snow.

Story

I know the white wedding dress is suicidal.
I know how the bride trembles, putting it on.

And tonight the groom is pissing into some shrubs
Behind a tavern.   It is late, and he thinks

Of twin sores riding the rump of a horse
As it is being whipped into a slow trot.

And of how the driver nods to the butcher, who waves
Back after smearing his apron with the blood

Of hogs. And now the butcher takes one long drink
Of black wine, and calculates how many new flies

Will hatch in the park, if there are three thousand
Flies in each pond, if there are thirty ponds.

Then he calculates how many each carp will eat.
If there are fifty carp in each pond. It passes

The day, he thinks, this calculating the flies.
Still, it is the butcher, slicing off his index finger

At the knuckle, who keeps death away from this poem
Long enough for the bride to marry. Long enough

For the horse to die, two months later, standing still
In a slaughterhouse. And long enough for the flies

To swarm over the meat in their loud, black weddings.

ELIZABETH LIBBEY

Spring And

five days five nights of rain, rush
of rain like one's own breathing, hurry,
new river through the meadow, go
and see, makes its bed over winter's
slicked-back grasses, spring's vivid stubble,
low-slung beech limbs, evergreen fractures,

crack and fall, run-off, road broken and
steaming like bread at the tables of
the God-fearing, earth thundering, I can't

help but think of Noah driving
home the last nail into sodden wood, drunk
on his own purpose, I don't know what
sort of creature I am that I was so worthy
of salvation, it's not the skin, the brain, maybe
potential: some exquisite gene I carry
in my tissue, am I future's hope, home
of the soul, God's crowning success?
It's hard to believe. No, if this

is the second coming of the great
deluge, I'll have to swim for it, God
must have learned something by now: that we
humans insist on living by the false
idol of our own sad wits, I'll swim
and gladly, going down with the ship of
my body, taking comfort from the pond
in the meadow, see? The harder it
rains, the quieter that pond grows, just

as if it exists in another dimension, and
that's where I'm going, concentrating
until this frenzied rain lulls me: I'm lying
in my bed, I'm that child in her bed, rain
softening roof's power to hold me in,
the animals all gather near as they should,
and we wait for God in his slick yellow raingear
to hand us down our sweet dreams,
hand us up clear of our breathing, give us a wink.

Come Into the Night Grove

These cedars don't hear
the little tune I hum, they tune
to the shift of bone against skin,

skin against air as I enter
the grove. I have not planned
a return, I don't turn
back toward you, waiting certain
as daylight, as
business unfinished.

It would startle you
to note how little of my face is left.
Already the eyes
have scattered among high leaves.
And this fever that nested
so reasonably in the cheek walls
careens, drunk animal, does
what it wants.

My body walks on
through the grove without me
as if it had purpose, a place
to get to. I do not. I am here,
distilled to fine mist
that hangs in the branches.
I am this ring around the moon. I try
to tell you: weather. Do not
be caught in the open.

Come into the grove. I want
to settle my facelessness
against yours. I want to say
nothing, remember nothing,
though yes I know always
someone stands at the edge of trees,
resisting entrance and by that resistance
yanking us back
into our shoes for our own sakes.

Do you stare after me
suspecting my body is a shell, a machine?
Do your eyes squint toward

some imaginary point of dark
on the far side of the grove where you believe
memory must turn me back
toward you? Listen. I remember
nothing, I have become the trees.
If you will not enter, stand still
a new way: roots, not resistance.
I breathe at you, I am nodding. Won't
you breathe back?
What we let go of with every pore is
what keeps us alive.

Juana Bautista Lucero, Circa 1926, to Her Photographer

I open up, mop gray ice
from the counter with my sleeve.
Place the pickles and eggs carefully before me.
December so suddenly: harsh
shadow, white sun. I, ninety-two
long as I remember.
And I unlock my door each morning
as if it were nothing. I watch
shadows against the door, how when wind comes,
they slide across the floor and up the counter
to my arm, how they curl into my palm
and when I turn there they are sprawled
along the wall. From this I know
all things pass through me.

The town comes to buy what I won't sell—
floursack apron on its peg, my
spotted hand. They want to have
something. A memento. They mistake me
for a man the way my nose has curled
under and my face darkened, but I'm more
legible with each sun, head sunk
into my thick neck. I wear

nothing that is mine. It is all
only a shadow caught in my head.

Mornings, I set my mirror
against the wrinkled window-glass and let
the sun dance however it will.
Evenings I turn that mirror on myself, bring
it close because I am no fool:
I am alive today for you. I fix
my hair, tie your bright scarf about my neck.
You want to hold a shadow, want the light
harsh and darkness filling up my eyes.
When I am frozen in myself, won't I grow
younger? Won't they look at me
a hundred years from here and know, was I
a woman or a man? Pick
the mirror up from the sill, and look and set
it down again. Let it, like any window,
have what it wants of dust.

Thomas Lux

Solo Native

Suppose you're a solo native here
on one planet rolling, the lily
of the pad and valley.

You're alone and you know
a few things: the stars are pinholes,
slits in the hangman's mask.
And the crabs walk sideways
as they were taught by the waves.

You're the one thing upright
on hind legs, an imaginer,

an interested transient.
Look— all the solunar tables
set with silver linen!

This is where you'll live, exactly
here in a hut on the green and gray belly
of the veldt. You'll be

a metaphor, a meatpacker,
a tree dropping or gaining
its credentials. You'll be

a dancer with two feet dancing
in the dirt-colored dirt. All this,
and after a few chiliads,

from your throat a noise,
an awkward first audible
called language.

Amiel's Leg

We were in a room that was once an attic,
the tops of the trees filled the windows, a breeze
crossed the table where we sat
and Amiel, about age four, came to visit
with her father, my friend,
and it was spring I think, and I remember
being happy— her mother was there too,
and my wife, and a few other friends.
It was spring, late spring, because the trees
were full but still that slightly lighter
green; the windows were open,
some of them, and I'll say it
out loud: I was happy, sober, at the time childless
myself, and it was one
of those moments: just like that Amiel
climbed on my lap and put her head back against my chest.
I put one hand on her knees

and my other hand on top of that hand.
That was all, that was it.
Amiel's leg was cool, faintly rubbery.
We were there—I wish I knew the exact
date, time—and that
was all, that was it.

Gold on Mule

On his knees with that pickaxe,
the sluice, the pan— all for a palm
full of dust. Valuable
eventually. Right now, the sun slams
on the wing of a fly
seeking moisture around the eye

of a mule waiting for his back
to be piled with gold. Poor bastard,
first he walks up here with sacks
of flour, beans, and sooner or later
leaves downhill, heavier, loaded.
It gets turned into money.

It's a sweat to get this stuff
and it's ugly from the rock.
The secret of minerals must be polish,
all the swipes of vanity applied
to what is really dirt. Rare
dirt, sure, but dirt on the spines

of mules— balanced like gold.
The man keeps digging, hacking out
a vein for what he needs: who
can name it? There's a slow shout,
nobody hears, in the air.
The man digs. The mule stares.

Barn Fire

It starts, somehow, in the hot damp
and soon the lit bales
throb in the hayloft. The tails

of mice quake in the dust,
the bins of grain, the mangers stuffed
with clover, the barrels of oats
shivering individually in their pale

husks— animate and inanimate: they know
with the first whiff in the dark.
And we knew, or should have: that day
the calendar refused its nail

on the wall and the crab apples hurling
themselves to the ground . . . Only moments
and the flames like a blue fist curl

all around the black. There is some
small blaring from the calves and the cows'
nostrils flare only once
more, or twice, above the dead dry

metal troughs. . . . No more fat tongues worrying
the salt licks, no more heady smells
of deep green from silos rising now

like huge twin chimneys above all this.
With the lofts full there is no stopping
nor even getting close: it will rage

until dawn and beyond,— and the horses,
because they know they are safe there,
the horses run back into the barn.

JACK MATTHEWS

Paradigm of a Hero

One memory I have from childhood
is this: a heavy man trudging
in boots, ahead of me, a lantern
bumping at his knee. I remember
stepping over railroad ties
and staring at his broad back
as he walked ahead; I remember
the smoky wake of his tobacco,
the sound of his boots clomping
in the cinders, remember tiredness,
the smell of lateness in the night . . .
I remember the darkness
which each step spilled him into,
though I forget who he was,
or why we were walking
on that cold night. I remember
the warm lantern clanking
against his leg, the darkness
all around, and the fact that
he never once paused, but stepped
like God himself, forward
into nothing, and into the past,
swinging his own casual light.

The Cheerleaders

Six girls in red skirts and red sweaters,
screaming by the field's pool table green
for the ghostly crowds on the grandstand hill
to print on silence their tumultuous will.

Six girls in short skirts and thick sweaters . . .
they are enthusiasms where thrilling dwells;

and in this dwelling, thrills almost love these
bright and sunny storms with hard and shiny knees.

What subsequence could justify such passion?
What happiness remains when the right team wins,
and the locker doors are closed, the boys sleeping,
and six silences lie in the midnight's keeping?

The People in These Houses

I'm not depressed, as I walk along this street,
by the age of these old houses; it's not their weight
of years that bothers me. The only vestiges
within their walls are of a material state:
wicker chairs, arthritic from thirty winters,
a sofa mildewed by the basement's weather,
and boxes filled with letters not worth saving.
I don't believe that here, in this stale climate,
ghosts live on to curse the merely living.
I fear another kind of curse that works inside,
worse than sin behind closed shutters,
that the people here are still more deeply haunted
by nothing, nothing in their hearts to hide.

Gravity's the Villain in This Piece

Gravity's the villain in this piece—
the laxness in the rose to slow decrease,
the tired instinct found within a man
for slumber at the noon . . . the dim plan
within the dog to lift his leg no more
and curl his brain around into his spoor.

Old men are apt to dream of being trees
and sprouting leaves from ears, and these
same leaves, no doubt, desire descent
into hard rock, and stones seek banishment

to air. All earthly things that yearn
to rise, tend sternly downward, turn
upon themselves and bite their minds
like mad dogs reeling. Upright signs
of growth are ever full of doubt,
and even children fill with dreams of not.

MEKEEL MCBRIDE

Loneliness

At first the pig is as tiny as a walnut
and so intelligent it answers the phone
taking messages in polite soprano.

She lets it move in, fills its bureau
with acorns, peppermint candies.

Its eyelashes are so long she has to comb them
daily. The pig grows quickly, pink moon,
never quite full.

It eats the dictionary, a kitchen chair,
her favorite hair brush. Even so,

she allows for it to stay, saying—
A simple case of domestic hunger that has its limits.
The pig continues to eat—

quilts, cooking spoons, the wedding dress
that she has not yet worn.

Eats and eats until it has to eat the living room,
the entire place. Picture this: a pig
as big as a five room apartment, grinning . . .

a woman wondering what to do next
when a little door in the pig's side swings open.

It is her dining room she sees inside,
the table neatly set for one, a candle and a rose,
glass platter of uncracked acorns, toy telephone.

The Going Under of the Evening Land

"But it should be quite a sight,
the going under of the evening land . . .
And I can tell you, my young friend,
it is evening. It is very late."

> — Walker Percy, The Moviegoer

In the evening land, a woman
places fresh bread on a polished table.
She turns on lamps, watching light
make golden maps on table top and parquet floor.
Here, without her knowing,
an interior continent completes itself.
She listens

to the glittery chatter of silverware
released from drawers that smell of Chinese tea.
Crows begin sleep now,
a few stars hidden in their pockets of black silk.
In the evening land
she considers how darkness leans cleanly
into its bright double—

how neither leaves for very long. Outside,
a child plays hide and seek with the rose bush
ghost. Now between light and dark,
the world splits open but only a little—
what is, what could be. And in this time
there are words that no one needs to speak:
                              I woke last night

thinking the bed to be an ocean liner
in touch with Antarctica, something
breaking up, something going under.
Tier on tier, the glittery necklace of the ship
sinking, or the iceberg singing, but I was
safe, I was safe and I
wanted you to know.

Red Letters

Hot-spit-and-damn of unchartable cargo flashes past
lightning blessed. Bridge shakes, almost shatters
with the passing. Gone, and then it's gone. Train

rumbling and plummeting out of summer air. Honest
in its passage, shakes bones, blooms hair. Seduces
and then stands you up, hopeless in one long whistle blast,

almost gets you there, getting and getting. Lackawanna
cars swollen with omniscient thunder, coffins, cheap
wine from Hungary. Gives you soot-stained wind,

a lust for the long worthless wheatfields of America.
Makes sealed baggage cars sing out their locked contents:
gladiola, apple, Aunt-So-and-So's black lace-up shoes,

a last letter from death row, nothing but snow
sealed under the silk skins of Maine potatoes. Shamelessly
invades the bedrooms of the unhappily married, inventing

their semi-tropical dreams of parole. Prudence, absent
even in the once-was-blue caboose. Won't be back
with its bereaved sheep grazing in the tiny meadow

of a boxcar next to the red letters of separated lovers.
Keeps no schedule, keeps nothing, and keeps going,
mad sweetheart to each steadfast tree it passes,

spits its way into the future, dragging with it
tracks and vantage point, sunset and perspective,
marries them all in a black daze of closed horizon

leaving only a slight sigh in the shaken trees, no birth
of storm, just ordinary dusk and the common burden
of having to admit that being witness was enough.

HEATHER McHUGH

In Light of Time

The names change,
the clock is a work of sparks
and I turn to a stranger

instead of you.
The light years pass.
The river burns. What once

was called Gondwanaland
is Cleveland now. The earth
is armed to the teeth,

the moon we face
is full of gravity,
attractive as indifference

and we are rolled or taken
for a ride. We can't
be otherwise, I'm not

myself, detaching
friends from their wristwatches,
touching off the haunted

metals in their eyes, affixing
pinwheels to their hats and heels.
In a flash they are gone.

WESLEY MCNAIR

House in Spring

Where it stands in the wind
unpinning the plastic
it has worn all winter

there is not one tree,
and nobody sees the long
remnants unfolding

in the late light.
Now it is tossing them
across its windowless

pair of shutters
and the great, swollen
place in the clapboards.

Now it is drawing them back
from the stairless
front door again

and again like an old
burlesque queen, alone
in the potato fields

of Mars Hill, Maine.

The Before People

There is a moment when they turn
to the ads that were meant for them
and are happy, a moment when the fat woman
thinks of melting her body away in seven days,
and the shut-in imagines big money
without leaving his home. Slowly,
as if for the first time, they read
the italics of their deepest wishes:
Made $5,000 in first month,
Used to call me Fatty, and all
the people with no confidence,
no breasts or hair in the wrong places
find pictures of the amazing results
in their own states. They have overlooked
the new techniques and the research
of doctors in Germany, they see that now,
suddenly so pleased they can hardly
remember being sad in this, their moment,
before, just before they lie back on the beds
of their small rooms and think about how foolish
they are or how farfetched it is or anything
except the actual photographs of their dreams.

My Brother Inside the Revolving Doors

I see you in Chicago twenty-five years ago,
a tall kid, surprisingly sure of yourself.
You have just arrived from the goat farm
to meet your father, the god you invented
after he left you in childhood.
It is the sunniest day you can remember,
and you walk the wide streets
of the city by his side in the dream
you have had all along of this moment,
except you are beginning to see how different
he looks, and how he does not care

about this in the same way that you do.
Which is when it happens, you are taken
inside the doors. Just like that
you are shut off from him, walking
in the weightlessness of your own fear.
And when you push your door, it leads
to other retreating doors, and again
and again, it takes you to the voice of him,
the fat man standing outside who has nothing
suddenly to do with your father and shouts
let go! let go! and you cannot let go.

JAY MEEK

The Week the Dirigible Came

After the third day it began to be familiar,
an analogue by which one could find
himself in finding it, so whenever it came
outside the window what came to mind was how
marvellous and common the day was, and how expert
I'd become at dirigibiles. And when
it stayed, one felt the agreeable confidence
that comes with having a goldfish
live four days. So I began to watch its shadow
passing through back yards, only once
looked at the tie-line swinging from its nose.
How much it seemed to want an effigy, a fish,
something that might save it from being simply a theory
about itself, and on the fifth day
old ladies came stomping out in their gardens
as the shadow passed under them,
and in the woods hunters
fired at the ground. The sixth day rained,
but morning broke clear and the air seemed grand
and empty as a palace, and I went out,

looked up, and the sun crossing my nose
cast such shadows as sun-dials make,
and I knew whatever time
had come was our time and it was like nothing else.

Vienna in the Rain

Dead center in the rain over Stephansplatz,
the cathedral is blackened
like the cone of something badly burned
in coming back to earth.

For a while I have stopped under the awning
of a clothing store
whose windows light up a display of dry shoes,
high on glass risers.
Walking in the rain after leaving the house

where Freud kept his quarters until the war,
I thought of him writing a friend
after his own operation for throat cancer,
"He'll live, but he won't sing."

Today I have walked through the small rooms
Haydn and Schubert left behind,
looking out a window
where their dear breaths once filled a day
with no less than song.

I wonder when I will begin to think of life
passing in the third-person,
when I already see myself going down a road
or stopping to dip my hand
in a fountain, the sailboats quietly moving.

How stunning it was on the train to Vienna
that moment in the mountains
we moved into a curve, during another rain,
when I saw our engine

enter a tunnel and I recognized what force

I was joined to, as though my next seconds
were suddenly inevitable, continuous,
which had felt separate from me

until then, when I wanted to see everything,
and I looked at the sheer face of the rock
with snow high in its crevices,
then I looked at the rain heavily falling,
and we went into the mountain
where deep in myself I did my best to sing.

A Walk Around the Lake

Two men are walking around the lake
in an open winter,
and as they walk toward a barn
it too seems round,
as though it were on fire,
or a concise miracle
around which cattle had gathered.
Hadn't they planned
to walk all the way around?
They seem content just to be going,
the snow is falling,
and if the seasons continue
as the men go on walking,
they will be walking the path
where hydrangea bloom,
and if they go ever so slowly
it will be next year, a new winter
when the miracle can happen,
the moment they step
into themselves, out of themselves.

Half-way around, they look toward
where they'd been

as if they'd walked around the cove
of a quarter-moon,
or sat turning a glass of ice-water
the way one turns an idea
of what is generous
until it clearly seems possible.
But over the barn door
there's a hex against strangers.
In back, a manure pile,
a broken wheel, the brown fields.
And from the evidence
architecture must be the science
of front and back,
vanity and neglect,
and history simply the debris
of what's already behind us:
czars, palace guards,
the shifts in power that come
from our having believed in sides.

If he were to go out walking,
the man who owns this barn,
perhaps he would think of going
to the other side, not around,
or if he took up with the men
he might see in the going round
how life gives itself to life,
and wherever they walk is home.

Walls

Being of sound mind, and in love with the child
who is becoming,

this is the testament I have written on my wall,
in the Tower, 1586:

Because I saw the world, and yet I was not seen,
I, Chidiock Tichborne,

give my blessing to the sweeps in our chimneys,
and to the truants

for their infinite capacity to rebound and grow;
my cares I give

to the pretty felons, and children in doorways,
for their cunning

and for their boundless impatience with the old.
I wish them well.

For being of stout heart, I have seen the world
is not boundless,

nor do the rivers flow through our countryside
for all time,

nor is age wisdom, nor shall hunger soon leave
the back door

before it comes swiftly knocking on the front.
Although in love

with the world, I remark upon its hard limits,
and pray the children

rejoice in their youth, as I have done in mine,
which was so good and free

and boundless, and far from where I lay my head
against the stone.

WILLIAM MEISSNER

After Going Off the Road During the Snowstorm

He still stares into the windshield.
He'd drive and keep driving
at 70, his vision
burning holes through decades
of blizzards.

His wife still clutches the dash
as if this skid across the slick surface
of winter will
never end.

After a few hours, the dome light's
glow shrinks, a
flashlight dropped
into a deep pool
of cloth. The radio
wraps itself in static,
a sound like footsteps
brushing across sand.

Now they can begin
the love dance
they have forgotten.
The back seat dreams
of the panting
that steams windows to silk.

In the dark they reach
to find each other
with that same joy a search party
feels, after days,
when it discovers the missing travelers
beneath a drift,

their pulsebeats
still jarring all the snow
from their wrists.

Twisters

What else is there to do but
aim his pickup into this fallow field
and spin?
The concentric ruts
are the circles under his eyes.
Dust devils curl behind the truck—
he imagines them swirling
like cyclones down Main Street,
tearing the tin grain elevator apart,
bringing the water tower to its knees.

He curses the grey screen that formed
between him and his woman last night—
the way she would only talk
through a locked hollow-core door,
his lips feeling the wood vibrate.

He cranks the wheel
until his elbows ache, accelerates
until his toes are blisters.
He believes dust will turn to gold,
believes he could spin and
spin, digging deeper into the land, spin
until he carves a shallow lake
in the center of this parched field, spin
the rest of his life,
but the engine
kills.

Climbing onto the hood,
he watches the last of the dust:
a small twister

the soft breeze tears apart
before it reaches the edge of town.

Leslie Adrienne Miller

My Students Catch Me Dancing

Only when I hear the knock
do I realize that what I've been doing
is probably odd: a few crooked pliés
and a variation on an arabesque
no dancer would recognize, after which
I arch my spine just to see
how far it will go, because it's spring
and my body's permutations are suddenly
as apparent to me as the shade
across the porch stair these two
young women ascend, glancing, as anyone would,
through the kitchen window to catch me
at the life I have without them.
When I open the door, they know better
than to giggle; they ask politely
if I *dance*, stretching the word
like a muscle to indicate art is meant.
They are not so much surprised by my dancing
as embarrassed to catch me concentrated
in my own grace, in the act of willing
myself beautiful. They would like
to apologize for something, but what?
Do you dance? one asks, as if I have
not been. *I have*, I say, as in not now,
not just now. They have seen how much
I liked the way my leg went up slowly
behind me, my breastbone forward, aloft
almost, as if a string were attached there.
They might have caught me at frying chicken

or sewing on a button; even trying faces
in the mirror would have been
less private, less sad, because I've said
too much about devotion, art, a whole life
concentrated in the movement of words
across a page, fingers across a keyboard,
so that the confinement of my dancing
to five square feet of dusk-lit kitchen
makes them too suddenly aware
of that place in us where art goes
when all the stages have gone dark.

The Weather of Invention

It is trying to be autumn in South Texas,
but the slender elms don't color well,
merely grow thinner wherever the wind
picks. I don't look too hard
for what's left because I need
soon, for the season to go dark,
all the honeysuckle a tangle of sticks
and empty nests, a November sky,
pale and functional as dimestore linoleum.
I came from a landscape of such fatalities.
Ohio's stubby hills scraped open and bled,
Indiana's crosshatch of stalks and mad
dogs, Missouri's Augusts prickled with drought
and my grandfather's nine wispy siblings.
There was always something to bear, or hide
or fight. Sometimes it was just
the weeds charging under the beans,
so we'd have to go low in uncle's
little plane and unfold the mist
of poison behind us. Sometimes
it was coyotes in the sheep,
and we'd have to wait for snow
so we could see their muddy hides loping

away from the steam fluttering above
the freshly dead lambs they left.

There isn't any nonsense about love
in a landscape like that, but winter
teaches the blood to run slow
so passion lasts a long time,
and the brilliant shock of the first
frost is as inevitable as the moment
when music stops and everyone
gets the closest chair, or none.
That's why the last time there were
nine inches of snow against my door,
and the face of a boy too young to keep
peered like the blurred moon at my window,
I let him in, raked the rime
from his hair, and pushed his chilly shirt
to the floor, ran warm palms under
his knees and shoulders till his breath
quickened and his nerves came to the surface.

It was as much as you'd do for a cold
barn cat you'd have to drown come spring
because it would get in the way
of something larger, a sow, a brood
mare, the warm wheel well of the pickup.
But when you know that the weather,
the wheat and the heart will all
come down at once, you learn
to stitch comfort out of husks,
to crack bliss out of stones, to coax
what you want out of what there is.

The Substitute

We knew only that she was too pretty
for 8th grade English, and that she'd had

a baby, but never a husband.
This gave us every right to moral outrage
and meanness. Somebody passed a note:
Nobody answer her, and we knew how
this worked, how the girls who swelled
a bit at the waist and took on that pale,
stricken look became invisible to us
soon after. Too pretty, too willing.
We wondered how the school could have missed
what we knew. This one with her great sheaf
of blonde hair bound in a silk scarf,
her hips and stomach returned to maiden
slimness did not fool us. We knew
the threads of story caught from the mouths
of mothers over the fence at the Country Club Pool,
whispers and glances when she came back
in the first bikini we'd seen on a woman,
and this only months after. *No good,* was all
my father said when I asked about the man
who left her. She was ours then,
for three weeks and a whole unit
of grammar. Simple choice: *was/were,*
she/her. We all looked out the window
at the mown hill, the adult world
driving down the afternoon; we traced
the hoops and lines of our games to keep
from looking into her eyes. Charlie
blew an obscene pink bubble, Shawn popped
her knuckles, and Kitty let go a whole
set of colored pencils. Somebody passing
in the hall squished their nose on the door
glass, and the substitute threw her hair
back over her shoulder like heavy brocade.
Chester panted, Pete squirmed and banged
the locks of his spine down the chair back.
She couldn't go to the principal,
she couldn't single out the intractable ones,
so she huffed, rolled her blue queen's eyes,
and answered the questions herself,

looking out above us somewhere,
and taking the tail of hair back
into her hands again and again: *lie/lay,*
she/her, he/him, while the chalk dust
gathered in pillars of sunlight: *ride/*
rode/ridden— We worked at our picture
of the man, swarthy, animal eyed, possibly
astride a motorcycle, cruelly muscled, steaming
bare chest. *Scum,* I thought, as I snuck
peeks at her creamy skin, the svelte navy skirt
she couldn't have worn when it happened.
I drew horses on all my notebooks,
swelling their withers and flanks,
topping them with girls who filled
their hands with streaks of mane,
blissful, reckless, while the substitute
went on invoking correct pronouns,
agreeing verbs, and *we/us, I/me*
dismantled her, her breasts, her lover,
her speckled scarves and dainty feet,
whatever we could conceive of her sex,
and carried it away in doodles, reveries,
silence, to the great cache of our rich
and dangerous unknowing.

LINDA MIZEJEWSKI

Parents Sleeping

My sleep in any city is still
the two-note pouring
of their breath, duet,
rhythm of the first rooms,
then hummed farther,
tremolo, down the hall,
the coalcars

rippling the dark
miles away.
Every passage safe,
I can sway, waved through,
carried out of light.

At the crossing I face
before dreaming wide,
I wait for them to pass:
in the stream of railcars
berthed, they sleep
in the dark compartment,
shuttled and obedient
as favorite shoes.
They would still be touched
awake by my cry,
come barefoot
in the unlit halls
to sing and make light.
But ready to fall unfastened
into the world opened
safe with their breath,
I let the gates rise,
let them go by.

Anaerobics: Elaine Powers, Wheeling, West Virginia

The karma of meringue,
the licked bowl, the pleated cheese
lip of casserole—

gels in the hollows,
or rises in gnarled loaves
of thigh. Slow

to loosen, the miners' wives
arch and wrench
on the butterfly machines

and boards; or stretched
as crossbows, fling out limbs
as if weight, like stoneshot,
could hurl to air.

Ten miles east and half mile down,
their men sweat black
in the crosscuts,
drill, explode, gouge out
what they can: tons
of dormant heat and light,
while its dust
bakes death in the lungs.

Breathless women,
plumbing the strata
of past sweetness,
we vanish together,
power in its great lumps
burning out of reach.
Tonight, the dream
will be hunger again,
yours and his,
the underground shaking
with the night shift on.

VERONICA MORGAN

Within the Greenhouse Effect

Tangled fine and light as our indecision
at the subway stop, a spring-like shower
fell in January. We didn't want to part.
We hadn't thought of being adulterers.

While rush hour muttered around us, rain
danced through your hair, sluicing the hot

choreography of your eyes and your mouth

with the first signs of thawing icecaps,
so I asked you to come with me down
those glistening streets where vendors
hawked, where whores yawned, and asphalt

rocked to throbbing underground trains,
where my knees melted as I led you deep
within the city, its glacial guilts,

back alleys breathless with chlorides,
dank with laundry years past whiteness
and steamed from ash can fires where
chestnuts, stolen, split darkly flowering.

Within the narrowest avenues of ourselves,
we put our lips to every neighborhood,
and our tongues to every food: papaya,

black-eyed peas and muscled briny turtle.
Now, under a seasonless sky, my mouth
waters with memory, again and again
with that narcotic spring of glaciers.

Still Life

With oxygen simmering and morphine peaking,
you sleep, as far as I can tell,
from my seat before the window view,

a Cezanne, flamed with raw leaves,
where boulders break the hillside surface,
their flashes of mica on mica intent

and dusky as our communication
dodging love by the timed coffee mugs
and primary colors of our past.

So often, that green-steeled desire
has caught us up short with one another.
Such history hardly matters now.

You'll wake to fuss about this child or that,
knock over the cough syrup, point out
the right Scrabble letter, up on the ceiling

and wonder about that steep hillside,
so distant, so near, like my dreams,
my holding what has never been and is always.

ED OCHESTER

The Relatives

Holidays, I'd look out the window for them
gathering like a flock of black-coated birds:
at Christmas, Fat Charlie, all red-faced and boozy,
he who always told jokes about outhouses and
parted his sparse hair down the middle;
crippled Marie, who didn't want to be a bother,
and Uncle George, the fierce fire chief and
Evelyn Number One with her warbling voice;
Lotte of the high Hungarian cheekbones,
who was beautiful and pious, and Uncle Arthur,
who did not always know where he was but is
the only one left of the old ones, 94 this week.

I want to name them all before they go utterly,
young women with gold at their breasts,
the men in their pride and small schemings,
songs after drink and the gossip,
old stories late into the night
as they praised their dead
as best they could, absolving

themselves with their repetitions
for never having had adequate words,
becoming thus, though clumsy,
like the *scop* in the meadhall,
like Nestor in the Pylian camp,
rescuing something from death, for the young,
for me, eating cakes with ginger ale,
listening, and it was all new:
the immigrants sailing in steerage to the New World—
"the ocean is big" my grandmother said,
who spent her whole life washing clothes—
the German builder of the bakery in Kingston,
the Wife Who Died From Grief When Her Husband Died,
the Son Who Supported His Mother and Three Brothers.

I never understood their sadness, I felt
a generation too late, at the edge of the world,
and when they left and walked out into the black
and under the street lamps on Woodhaven Blvd.
it was as though they were walking through spotlights
the way Jimmy Durante did on television
at the end of the program slowly walking,
his back bent, from spotlight to spotlight
stopping at each to turn and wave and
walk again into an infinite regression
of lights, turning and waving,
kissing goodbye.

All I have left for my children
who never knew them are a few stories
and an image of a long parade,
George and Sybil, Charles, Ernest
who always smelled of kerosene,
little people joining the famous
in shrinking as they go backward
through the abyss with the others,
older, all traveling: Ruprecht,
Harthacnut, Wang-Wei, and before them,
Arzes, Sextus Marcius, waving and bowing,

Praxithea, Agathocles, an immense crowd
kissing and walking away
until each is tiny as
one neuron or gone.

The Canaries in Uncle Arthur's Basement

In the white house in Rutherford
the ancient upright piano never worked
and the icy kitchen smelled of Spic 'N Span.
Aunt Lizzie's pumpkin pie turned out green
and no one ate it but me and I did
because it was the green of the back porch.
That was the Thanksgiving it rained and I first thought
of rain as tears, because Aunt Lizzie was in tears
because Arthur came home from the soccer game drunk
and because he missed dinner, brought a potted plant
for each female relative, and walked around the table
kissing each one as Lizzie said "Arthur, you
fool, you fool," the tears running down her cheek as
Arthur's knobby knees wobbled in his referee's
shorts, and his black-striped filthy shirt wet from the rain
looked like a convict's. What did I know?
I thought it meant something. I thought
no one would ever be happy again. I thought
if I were Uncle Arthur I'd never again
come out from the dark basement where he raised canaries,
the cages wrapped in covers Aunt Lizzie sewed,
and where, once, when I was very small and because Uncle
    Arthur
loved me or loved his skill or both he slowly removed the cover
from a cage and a brilliant gold bird burst into song.

New Day

Yes, the sun rises an angry red,
what the Romans called *oriens*,

what the religious associate with Christ,
and I walk out in my shorts, stretching
and puffing to train the scarlet runner beans
to their trellis; whatever god governs
beans has smiled, the vines grown
a foot overnight, and as I lace them
around the nervous network of twine
my son, who last night collapsed
in an anguish of stertorous breathing
comes down, stretches and yawns, pees.
Pots rattle in the kitchen,
grits and eggs,
and the rooster with a pneumonic lung
croaks—oohgggHHH—for the sun
but he hasn't died yet and
as I'm eating, the radio says
the President is lobbying
to subvert another small country
and I flip the dial and a preacher
who knows nothing says that except
for one thing there is nothing to know,
and when I walk out again
a hummingbird's in the salvia,
the sun's up, the dog on his chain
whines for breakfast, and the squash
are flourishing and when I stand near them
with my bright yellow shirt the cucumber beetles,
who love anything yellow, land on me and
are destroyed, sinners on the shirt
of a jealous god, and the sun's rising
to zenith, the chickens are scratching
around in their mud and if you
were very young you could say
this is heaven what with the dew
and the birds chirpy and all and yes
if you wait long enough
you will see the new moon
with the old moon in her arms.

MARY OLIVER

At Blackwater Pond

At Blackwater Pond the tossed waters have settled
after a night of rain.
I dip my cupped hands. I drink
a long time. It tastes
like stone, leaves, fire. It falls cold
into my body, waking the bones. I hear them
deep inside me, whispering
oh what is that beautiful thing
that just happened?

Morning at Great Pond

It starts like this:
forks of light
slicing up
from the horizon,
sailing over you,
and what's left of night—
its black waterfalls,
its craven doubt—
dissolves like gravel

as the sun appears
trailing clouds
of pink and green wool,
igniting the fields,
turning the ponds
to plates of fire.
The creatures there
are dark flickerings
you make out

one by one
as the light rises—
blue-winged herons,
wood ducks shaking
their bright crests—
and knee-deep
in the purple shallows
a deer drinking:
as she turns

the silver water
crushes like silk,
shaking the sky,
and you're healed then
from the night— your heart
wants more, you're ready
to look and look,
to hurry anywhere,
to believe in everything.

An Old Whorehouse

We climbed through a broken window,
walked through every room.

Out of business for years,
the mattresses held only

rainwater, and one
woman's black shoe. Downstairs

spiders had wrapped up
the crystal chandelier.

A cracked cup lay in the sink.
But we were fourteen,

and no way dust could hide

the expected glamour from us,

or teach us anything.
We whispered, we imagined.

It would be years before
we'd learn how effortlessly

sin blooms, then softens,
like any bed of flowers.

The Rabbit

Scatterghost,
it can't float away.
And the rain, everybody's brother,
won't help. And the wind all these days
flying like ten crazy sisters everywhere
around can't
seem to do a thing. No one but me,
and my hands like fire,
to lift him to a last burrow. I wait

days, while the body opens and begins
to boil. I remember

the leaping in the moonlight, and can't touch it,
wanting it
miraculously to heal and spring up
joyful. But finally

I do. And the day after I've shoveled
the earth over, in a field nearby

I find a small bird's nest lined pale
and silvery and the chicks,

are you listening, death? warm in the rabbit's fur.

ROSALIND PACE

Tingel-Tangel

from a handcoloured lithograph, 1895, by Edvard Munch

It's the high kick they wait for, not quite allowing
themselves to be breathless, those proper men,
sliding into the dance hall after hours with their
pockets full of coins, their ties straightened,
and their tongues safely hidden behind their teeth
where they can move in the dark searching
for language they know will never be tender.
And then it comes, the high kick, the sudden flash
of white petticoats. The bare upper thighs. The
fleeting vision of treasure in the heart of the
tropics, a flash of sweet sweat and musk and powder;

it's harmless, after all. Nothing to tell
their wives about, just performer and audience,
two distinct line-ups, the women seated across
the stage waiting their turn, their legs not crossed
but open like the gates to a tunnel one dreams
of driving through to a country so foreign it
almost seems like home. Madame comes to the men
like a mountain, her bosom bare as a rock and as
formidable. What man would be able to climb that white
cliff and what man doesn't want to prove himself there.

The women are dressed in red, black, and yellow,
no soft colors of the natural world, and yet
this scene is not unnatural— see how the women
smile and frown at the same time, open their legs
and keep their arms locked in their laps,
and how the men, even from the back, seem like
well-scrubbed schoolboys taken to assembly, settled
in the front row and told to behave, and how madame's
great front looms over them. Just in case.

This Is English and I Am Speaking It No Matter What

The air is filled with apple blossoms and rain
and new leaves show their pale undersides.
I have no money, no job, no love, and seven
more phone calls to make and none of that
matters as much as these leaves and the way
they hang on. Who am I trying to fool?

Only one car has come down this street
in the last hour and I thought I loved
this solitude, but I don't.

Two friends in the last two days have put
their heads in my lap and said I just want
to find me a beautiful young thing
who will smile all the time and
take care of me and who doesn't
speak English.

What do I make all these words for,
if not for love?

In the silence I made before I told them
exactly what I thought of their visions,
I stood once again on a green hill
and preached to the invisible multitudes
of my childhood
and the branches of the trees bent over
and the wind took the blossoms off
in a single exhalation
and everything revealed itself without shame,
even the new leaves, and the voices,
and my open, empty hands.

LINDA PASTAN

Because

Because the night you asked me,
the small scar of the quarter moon
had healed— the moon was whole again;
because life seemed so short;
because life stretched before me
like the darkened halls of nightmare;
because I knew exactly what I wanted;
because I knew exactly nothing;
because I shed my childhood with my clothes—
they both had years of wear left in them;
because your eyes were darker than my father's;
because my father said I could do better;
because I wanted badly to say no;
because Stanley Kowalski shouted "Stella . . .";
because you were a door I could slam shut;
because endings are written before beginnings;
because I knew that after twenty years
you'd bring the plants inside for winter
and make a jungle we'd sleep in naked;
because I had free will;
because everything is ordained;
I said yes.

At Home

The secret strangers
in my house
help with the dishes,
smile for the camera.
When the pictures are developed
there is no one there.
They nod vaguely when I question

turning my sound down low.
At the table they break,
break my bread.
I never guess
it is the loaf
of exile.

RICARDO PAU-LLOSA

Ostiones Y Cangrejos Moros

For what seemed to be the whole night
he burned, an effigy on the coast
commemorating the day of St. John. It stood

above a pyramid of trash, itself made of trash,
his jewels falling to the pyre at its feet,
the glow eclipsing night and Havana.

The flames increased the giant and all around
people stood at a safe distance and gazed,
a human halo watching a flame the shape of a man,

a man turning into a constellation. That morning
I had seen on the dog tooth rocks of the coast
a nation of urchins and among them mollusks and crabs

clinging as best they could or dancing upon the charge
of broken tide, the sea rising and falling like breath
in the dreamer's chest aspiring life into a flesh

whose mind was lost. Did the mollusks dream the terror
of the tides around them, and could that dream bring
safety into these shells gripped one to another and to rock?

The dreamer knows he is on fire and that his flames

catch on the wet black concaves of the mollusks and blind
the crabs' tiny orbs, their minute claws snapping

at the misplaced appearance of the sun. With each breath
the flames grow and break into a thousand brief stars
toward the sea. The world burns, it's true,

but he is serene. In the charred morning
he will walk among the tiniest lives that circle him.
Already we lift our eyes and arms to him in welcome.

Frutas

Growing up in Miami any tropical fruit I ate
could only be a bad copy of the Real Fruit of Cuba.
Exile meant having to consume false food,
and knowing it in advance. With joy
my parents and grandmother would encounter
Florida-grown *mameyes* and *caimitos* at the market.
At home they would take them out of the American bag
and describe the taste that I and my older sister
would, in a few seconds, be privileged to experience
for the first time. We all sat around the table
to welcome into our lives this football-shaped,
brown fruit with the salmon-colored flesh
encircling an ebony seed. "Mamey,"
my grandmother would say with a confirming nod,
as if repatriating a lost and ruined name.
Then she bent over the plate,
slipped a large slice of *mamey* into her mouth,
then straightened in her chair and, eyes shut,
lost herself in comparison and memory.
I waited for her face to return with a judgement.
"No, not even the shadow of the ones back home."
She kept eating, more calmly,
and I began tasting the sweet and creamy pulp
trying to raise the volume of its flavor
so that it might become a Cuban *mamey*. "The good

Cuban *mameyes* didn't have *primaveras*," she said
after the second large gulp, knocking her spoon
against a lump in the fruit and winking.
So at once I erased the lumps in my mental mamey.
I asked her how the word for "spring"
came to signify "lump" in a *mamey*. She shrugged.
"Next you'll want to know how we lost a country."

Ganaderia

Stories have it that when the rebels
descended on Camaguey province they ordered
the cattle slaughtered to feed the campesinos.
Neither the industry nor the cattle ever recovered.
The guerrilla leaders were educated men,
how could they not know you don't eat breeding stock?
Two decades later Fidel is in love with a cow,
Ubre Blanca (White Udder). Before the cameras
he explains each step of his gloved penetration,
bull semen dripping from his fist. Gently he lifts
Ubre Blanca's tail after reassuring her
with a stroke on the rump. The forearm sinks
into the cow slowly and his face announces
the moment he opens his fist inside her.
One day the record breaking milk mother died
and a distraught Fidel ordered a monument be built
to White Udder, the revolutionary cow.

Fidel's parents finally married to get him
into the Jesuit school in Oriente. The bovine
mother, the stern father, illegitimate Edmund
pulling a revolver against his rival's head
in a café, the autonomous University his hideout.
He married the convenient daughter of a *batistiano*.
In exile former classmates will talk of his brutality,
but none opposed him when he descended from the *Sierra*.
They were educated men, how could they not know
what was coming? How could they not save *Ubre Blanca*
from the endless speeches, the cameras, and the fist?

The Island of Mirrors

"The objects we look at produce very perfect images at the back of our eyes."

— Descartes, "Dioptric"

The dream where land
breaks like surf
cannot be dreamt.
Such a dream would pull
the anchor from the heart
and set the world adrift
like a plague ship,
the rats turning into words.

Take the dream,
the fertile dream of an eye,
and take a dead man's eye,
remove the membranes around it
(all this in your dream)
and replace the membrane
with eggshells. Hold
the eye in a light
tidal with images.
They will awaken on the shells.

Take the little world
of safety in places that bear us.
An island bore me, a land
filled with double mirrors,
so that it was no longer
an island but a space
memory resolves to leave us in
like an infant bundle.
The only real space
lives in a dead man's eye.

ANNE S. PERLMAN

Summer Adjustments

1

Go softly now in the presence of circles,
along the low marsh roadway
between blackbirds and gulls:
in the sticky wind of the valley
wings are brushing.

2

Now we are passengers
bunched in a foreign train
compartment (no matter the country).
Our strangeness breaks over us,
crowded against
a man and a woman
in love. They are together
inside the circle of their shoulders.
It's the talk (no matter the language)
so close, so freighted
the circuit is closed.
Outside their brilliant territory
                              we dwindle.

3

Motionless in the August heat
we notice the shadow on the sundial,
how it curves through the weather.
Our heads turn to the sun's glare,
taste the heat wasting in our mouths.

Survival

This love
is our own mix . . .
a given,
like the rose I find
in a rough fall of pine cones . . .
or a single kite spool
here in our hands,
its twine unwinding
up the drafts
over light settling
red on an iron mountain.
And on toward the harshness of stars
rounding the sky.

It is this knowing
I have a stubborn
glittering ally . . .
who will vouch
I passed this way.

At Fifty in the Crystal-Dead Eye of the Center

A mare, my head cocking back
to see the meadow pass below,
I skin the trees at a canter,
hind feet skew out
to the soft cliff-edge.

At last a brittle beach,
and overhead,
swallows flanking swallows.
Oh, praise the Lord with rue!

Only the slide alone, now,
down the scoured sides
of sand dunes,
sifting on a wrist of wind.

Family Reunion

All right. Let's hear it
for this fine figure of a
trout on every plate.
In front of me on white china
his fry-dark belly
dark as my own bones,
closet bones
that will never see light.

Now then,
cut off his head.
The quick guillotine
at the quieting table.
Slit the thin skin,
lay back two neat
sections of flesh,
the vertebrae intact.
There'll be no thrust and parry
of his bones darting in my throat.

Flip the body
to repeat on his underside.
The spine lifts out easily.
White how white
its bones are.
Do I have any part
of me left,
whole and shiny?
These secret fish bones
have no cracks.

Against the brittle talk
breaking up the table,
I lay that trout's
perfectly branching core
by its blind head
at the rim of my plate.

JOYCE PESEROFF

Bluebird

My mother's voice is at my throat
—"Try a scarf in the neckline"—
and on my lips: "Just a little
lipstick." Today I'm wearing both.

My "mother's voice," pitched high, carries
reprimand and care:
"No boom on the table!" My daughter
swats me as I carry her

away from the dearest
activity on earth— sticks, stones, struck
as if the coffee table were a flint.

"Barbarian," I croon
in heels. "What's that?" she asks and rips
a nylon with a fingernail.

She cries at the turtleneck
pulled over her head. "I'll give you something
to cry about!" I hush, succeeding for another

day, or an hour— another minute
late for work. Tonight I'll choose
a lullaby: "Bluebird
at my window," Mother sang to me,
a voice that could broom sorrow

through the door . . . A decal
staggered on the painted bureau,
blue wing seeking, finding no way out.

Adolescent

I wandered lonely as a dog
avoiding trouble,
and others of her species,

while daffodils like gold stars
(for good behavior)
rebuked me, and lilac buds

in phallic clusters,
doubling size each day.
I kept my nose to the curb,

never to the grindstone,
like someone looking for money
down a sewer-grate. Depressing,

isn't it, when buses grind past—
not one going where you're going,
the crowd at your back

revving its discontent
as if *you* were leader of the pack.
A Coke bottle tinkles, hurled

rocks ripple the civic
display of daffodils.
You watch Coke drip

into the gutter, livening
a party of ants,
their frenzied dancing—

better to wander, quickly,
away, before the soft
wow of police cars

climbs rapidly up the scale
of urban music . . .
O William, what common

memories stir our yelps in the dark?

A Dog in the Lifeboat

*". . . (a number of) normal, adult humans and a dog will all
die unless one of the humans sacrifices his life, or one of
the humans or the dog is thrown overboard."*

— Tom Regan, *discussing* The Case for Animal Rights

Harry, who is allergic, offered to chuck him
over the side, for how could they share water
with such droolery, sour baby-
pink tongue drooping like a second sad
tail? Angelica needed to know if Rover,
coffled with his master, could be said
to have joined the pirogue "willingly."
The mother ship bleeped in the blue,
heeling like a sow— tremoloed, and was gone.
What a fix! Jerome's first cruise, begun
so airily, his fiesta hat fringed with little
red balls, like Auntie's curtains— now,
so bare, and with a feckless canine to boot.
He brooded and voted—surely this was classic
democracy?—with Harry. The pup, requiring more sleep,
drummed his feet appealingly. The boat swayed
on the wind's samba. The last ship's biscuit—
why, this is almost like dog biscuit,
Angelica mused—was distributed by our self-
proclaimed Captain. Hmmm, I wonder if
this is autocratic, Harry whispered to Jerome.
The dog, refreshed, wagged his tail
upsetting Captain's carafe— now look
what you've done! Council immediately convened.
Either that animal goes, said Harry—

need I say what furor developed,
what hubbub? Careful, we may capsize!
Opinion divided; the stern Captain, seated
athwart the bow, decided, Star-Chamber-wise—
against. So Rover, condemned to walk the plank,
was last seen paddling toward Death as we all eventually do.

ADORA PHILLIPS

The Summer My Mother Fell in Love and Wanted to Leave My Father

The safety light seeps
into father's space, his shadow
and eyes, when he walks outside
to see if the moon lights
the far meadow, and the porch
where she stands, wanting
and not wanting to leave.

He thinks, *In the winter,*
I'll still see light
from another house
through sparse bare trees
in the back yard.
Under a moon, the long blue
hills seem to change.
He sucks ice cubes dry,
stepping into the intoxicated

embrasure of memory: old desire.
Puzzled by the many things
which speed up, and slow down.
How the earth may curve fast enough
to make a man sick.
He enjoyed being alone

with her. The strange
shape of her humour.

She's pacing on the front porch
when he walks to the kitchen
for more whiskey. Her movement,
always clumsy, tears
the summer night. A foot dragging,
hands thumping between rail space.
From inside the screen door
he wills to her
Turn around. Turn

around, please.
Whiskey pinning his nerves
he's memory and apology at once—
tongue-tied and awkward
when he climbs the stairs,
imagining he moves fast enough
to catch her fall
from his push.

Photograph & Story in The Press: *The Mother Whose Children Burned to Death*

She isn't straight.
A pew pins her to the husband
she stopped knowing. He
had drifted into uneasiness,
sometime, somewhere. I understand
life became sad. Her arms
are suspended. Face,
clenched. Eyes, elsewhere
from the moment.
She was always lost. Loss
caught her in this story.

CAROL J. PIERMAN

How We Learned About Friction

A pink eraser rubbed to shreds
or chewed until our teeth got hot.
A sandy taste. The teacher said,
Brush your erasures from your desks.

We rubbed like insects sang,
wiping out the lopsided cow,
the silent letter, the incorrect
capital for Idaho. We learned
from our mistakes.

And then we applied our knowledge,
sharpening popsicle sticks behind
the gym. Friction was the fire
we started, smoke loping toward
the bus garage. We rubbed it out.

We squeezed our sweaty legs
while she scolded us from her desk.
She talked and talked. We rubbed
her out. We stared out the window
until it was spring.

Friction was in our hands when
we rubbed them together, plotting
revenge. And it was in the rusty
swingset chains we wrapped around
the ringing poles.

Friction made our voices shrill.
Even when we tried to whisper,
it gave us away. And when we rubbed
our papers black, spit
brought them back to life.

Pilgrims

You could tear off a piece of road
and chew it like Black Jack gum
the day we went to the junkyard—
past Slaughterpen Road, past Fuquay
Varina, farther south than we'd ever
been—to buy a seatbelt for the Maverick.

Hubcaps were piled around the gate
like prostheses at some Catholic
shrines. The nuclear family in the
office showed us on the chart
where to find the Fords, then
the youngest son opened the back
door and pointed us down an alley
of calamity and shattered glass.

The geckos raced from us like skinny
hens, and we followed their flail
tracks through the pink dust
to the Mustangs, Pintos, and LTDs.
If Henry Ford could have seen it,
he would have worked harder
on the soybean car.

Every car we had ever known was there:
the Corvair, smooth as a kidney bean,
the cruel El Camino, the last Rambler—
and all the family sedans that went crazy
at the crossroads and the EMS
came running with the Jaws of Life.

They all looked as if they had been
thrown, or dropped from great heights.
Tires were torn, filled with black
water and breeding mosquitoes.
The smell of sex was as strong
as the smell of death. Weeds grew

through the cracked vinyl seats,
up through the festive combs
and parts of sunglasses. And
there were black pennies that
no one would spend or ever save.

The sun went dark, the way it gets
in an eclipse—brown, and bright
at the edges—and the air smelled old,
greasy like the coveralls that hung
for years on the basement hook.
Oil soaked into the red dirt, and I
sat, right there in Kentucky,
head between my knees, watching
the ground come up, braced to survive
any crash— no belt cinching me
to the fragile structure of life.

Eight Cows

*"Sometimes I would like to
forget all this, buy a small farm
and take care of eight cows."*

> — *a victim of burnout*

What would I do without you?
You have reminded me of cows,
their awkward shapes in which
they seem so terrifyingly to float.
You have reminded me of the cows
of my childhood. The steaming
barn in the dark morning,
the soft crunching of the straw,
a large eye rolling while my father
emptied the udders, while I poked
at the hide trying to figure out
what it was that it was stretched
over. Surely not flesh,
not blood and nerves, but something

like milk, before it becomes milk,
small cows in small barns.

I can hardly drive through the countryside
without pulling up at the dairy
farms, staring out at the fields
as if cows were relics
of a lost past. The brindle cow
who lies on her side, will she
ever get to her feet again? The mystery
of the four stomachs, the cud,
the cow flops I once followed
to the river when I was six
and we hadn't raised cows
for a year. If you look away
from a cow, she grows invisible,
becoming part thistle, part cloud.
When cows gallop to the barn at night
they fill like sails, dewlaps swinging,
a fleet of good girls, coming home
across the fluttering bay.

Lawrence Raab

The Room

Everything has been arranged too carefully.
The way the eyes are closed, that certainty.
I can see it isn't possible to pretend
that the dead are only sleeping.
The way the hands are folded
we don't have to touch them.
When I touched them I knew it wasn't necessary.
I've watched my wife and daughter sleeping.
I've watched you. No matter how still,
there's an imperceptible trembling

accompanies everything that lives.
It's the way a feather sways, that chance.
It's the cloud on the mirror,
that stain. For a while we imagined
our concerns were yours. Is this blue dress
the one you would have wanted to wear?
And these rings, that silver pin?
Is this the music you especially liked to hear?
But the dead among their flowers
have no preferences, and I think
it must be wrong to pretend otherwise,
if only for my sake, and not now for yours.

The Witch's Story

Everything you have heard about me
is true, or true enough.
You shouldn't think
I'd change my story now.
A stubborn, willful little girl
comes sneaking
around my house, peering
in all the windows. She's disobeyed
her parents, who knew
where the witch lived. "If you go,
you're not our daughter any more."
That's what they told her. I have
my ways of knowing. All pale
and trembly then, she knocks at my door.
"Why are you so pale?"
I ask, although of course
I know that too.
She'd seen what she'd seen—
a green man on the stairs, and the other one,
the red one, and then the devil himself
with his head on fire, which was me,
the witch in her true ornament, as I
like to put it. Oh, she'd seen what she needed

to send her running home
but she walked right in, which is the part
I never understand completely. Maybe
she believed, just then,
that she was no one's daughter anymore,
and had to take her chances, poor thing,
inside with me. "So you've come
to brighten up my house,"
I said, and changed her into a log.
It was an easy trick, and gave me little pleasure.
But I'd been waiting all day.
I was cold, and even that
small fire was bright, and warm enough.

For You

for Judy

I don't want to say anything about
how dark it is right now, how quiet.
Those yellow lanterns among the trees,
cars on the road beyond the forest,
I have nothing to say about them.
And there's half a moon as well
that I don't want to talk about,
like those slow clouds edged
with silver, or the few unassembled stars.
There's more to all of that than this,
of course, and you would know it
better than most, better I mean
than any other, which is only
to say I had always intended
finding you here where I could
tell you exactly what I wanted to say
as if I had nothing to say
to anyone but you.

On the Island

After a night of wind we are surprised
by the light, how it flutters up from the back of the sea
and leaves us at ease. We can walk along the shore
this way or that, all day. Sit in the spiky grass
among the low whittled bushes, listening
to crickets, to the whisk of the small waves,
the rattling back of stones. "Observation,"
our Golden Nature Guide instructs, "is the key to science.
Look all around you. Some beaches
may be quite barren except for things washed up."
A buoy and a blue bottle, a lightbulb
cloudy but unbroken. For an hour
my daughter gathers trinkets, bits of good luck.
She sings the song she's just invented:
Everybody knows when the old days come.
Although it is October, today falls into the shape
of summer, that sense of languid promise
in which we are offered another
and then another spell of flawless weather.
It is the weather of Sundays,
the weather of memory, and I can see
myself sitting on a porch looking
out at water, the discreet shores
of a lake. Three or four white pines
were enough of a mystery, how they shook
and whispered, how at night I felt them
leaning against my window, like the beginning
of a story in which children must walk
deeper and deeper into a dark forest,
and are afraid, yet calm, unaware
of the arrangements made for them to survive.
My daughter counts her shells and stones,
my wife clips bayberry from the pathway. I raise
an old pair of binoculars, follow the edge of the sky
to the lighthouse, then down into the waves as they
fold around rocks humped up out of the sea.
I can turn the wheel and blur it all

into a dazzle, the pure slips and shards of light.
"A steady push of wind," we read in the book,
"gives water its rolling, rising and falling motion.
As the sea moves up and down, the wave itself
moves forward. As it nears the shore friction
from the bottom causes it to rise higher
until it tips forward in an arc and breaks."
On the table in front of the house
is the day's collection: sea-glass
and starfish, a pink claw, that blue bottle—
some to be taken home, arranged in a box,
laid on a shelf, later rediscovered, later
thrown away, casually, without regret,
and some of it, even now, to be discarded,
like the lesser stones, and the pale
chipped shells which are so alike
we can agree that saving one or two will be enough.

Thomas Rabbitt

My Father's Watch

From Boston south he talks of citrus fruit
And extra children who pop like extra toes.
A good man cuts them off or he makes room.
His girlfriend looks like she will never laugh.
There is an old man who lived in shoes,
Refinished basements, plastered catacombs
Where the cold walls felt like a dead son's face.
Sons are lemons: yellow, sour, small and tough.
Atlantic City. We stop to play roulette.
Chamber to chamber our winnings grow.
Next day, the pike Russia, the pavement slick,
He tells her: in the basement room my son
And I held pistols to our heads and played
For laughs. His world outside of time is charmed.

In Delaware no child has ever died.
We stop in Baltimore to buy the watch.
He knows which street. From alley to alley,
Block to block, he hears it tick. The harbor rolls.
When wound my father's watch goes *click*.
The sound the bottom makes before it drops
And the Oldsmobile skids into Florida.
British frigates are bombarding Fort McHenry.
His luggage, his bankbook, his girlfriend and I
Spill into the sunshine. Now he is retired.
His yellow watch carries him, every nervous tick
Counting the walls of each new empty room.

Tortoise

I guess today's another day among the days
When nothing ever happens well,
Another afternoon lost drinking, rocker
Jammed against the front porch wall.
Spring. And it has just stopped raining. Two boys
Come loping up the muddy road.
The boys decide to stop, unload their load,
A turtle on the porch for me to praise,
Which I do, I do, box turtle, which they say
They found abandoned and alone
And nearly dead beside the road
And will I let them put it in my pond.
I will. I do. And when, just like a stone,
It sinks and does not rise again, I say,
Don't worry, turtles always sink this way.
The boys spend hours watching and I sit back
To drink my beer. The ducks raise hell. The sun
Setting lights up the water while the boys
Gaze out over the pond. They shake their heads
And take this as their loss. Yes, I can lie.
Yes, I will tell them what I do not know.

For Those Who Will Live Forever

The law said Dale Booth died of falling.
Some nights Dell Booth sits at home and drinks.
His wife talks on. Dell sits and stares
Through the thin pane of his picture window
Down through the burned pines to the highway.
He thinks that everyone is moving away.
The glass shakes. Dale Booth died at two,
Aged two, at two in the morning, of falling
When Dell, falling, could not bear the screaming
And pulled the blocks from beneath his son's end
Of their mobile home. Some nights, late, Dell thinks
He hears a child calling from the tall goldenrod
Near the roadway. *Sorry. Sorry.* But it is only
A possum or dog some car has killed.

PAULA RANKIN

To the House Ghost

Just because I turn on the light
it doesn't mean I don't want you around.
I know how you like to keep your own
shredded space among hangers and vents;
you think I have no room for you
at the table or in bed. But listen:
I have made room in my ribcage more than once.
There is always something that wants to move over
to borrow air like trouble.

You could light my cigarettes.
After I'm in bed, lean over my impossible wishes
and blow them out. Lie down and tell me
who cut you down in your prime,
describe the weapon.

Fifteen

To fit in, I lifted "Angel Baby"
from the rack of 45s, slipped it
inside my coat, walked out of the drugstore
with Susan and Irene. Within the week,
my life turned serious: my boyfriend
dumped me, the woman at the drugstore
called Susan's mother, who called Irene's,
agreeing I was too bad
to hang out with. It wasn't fair: I didn't even like the record:
    Susan
and Irene had drawers jammed with stolen nailpolish, lipsticks,
mascara. They did it all the time;
they did *it* all the time.

And so I was alone.
And so I smashed the record, threw its shards out,
promised God *never, if only* . . .

And so I made up a boyfriend
from another town and bought myself
a rhinestone ring at Woolworth's. I swooned
to him half the night on the phone,
I went to his Prom, did it
on the back seat of his Chevrolet.
Soon I would be pregnant, disgraced. My first child
would look just like her father, spend her life
searching for him.

In the girls' room, Susan and Irene
asked me to take off my ring,
let them test it against mirror glass.
it slashed a path across our faces.
It must be real, Susan said to Irene.
It must be real, Irene said to Susan.

Bedtime Story

If the Devil don't want nothing
he must want something.

If he ain't barely imaginable
he must be red fluorescent skin,
spikes jutting from forehead,
a shredded grin, as in *gnashing of teeth*.

If he seen you
it's too late.

But hide, hide under the covers,
may be he gets confused
in his tenses
and agreements. May be
he thinks you signed something
when you ain't signed nothing at all.

Tell him you can't hardly write.

Two Lovers on Bridge in Winter

It is not clear what they love,
as they lean over the rail
in opposite directions

staring across the blue ice.
Where snow sleeves the pilings,
there are tiny tracks pricked

like maps for ascent, but there are no
birds in the picture. The sky
is immense, and has the pallor of skin

in nursing homes. In the foreground,
frozen branches scratch the air:

pine boughs look as though, any moment,

they will give up their luggage of snow
and crash through bridge, lovers, lake.
The lovers' stares make fissures

and hairline cracks in the dream
of walking on water. They are so tiny,
set against all that will happen!

I move in close and ink third arms
for both of them, placing them
hand over hand to clutch the same span

of railing before the wind
picks up, and snow buffs its slow erasures.
I swivel their profiles and have them embrace

for all whose dreams crack
like ice thawing. See how carelessly

they breathe
or hold their breath.

For the Obese

We are always saying,
with will power,
their buttons would slip into holes
over their bellies, their zippers
would close like a mouth
which gets the last word
in the old argument
of why some eat to stay alive
while some eat to summon impossible lovers
who fill every inch of the body.

Then we say it's hard to find their eyes
or the stand their bones take

so far underground.
We lock them into their bodies,
slipping the key into our pocket,
fingering it from time to time
as reminder of those few wars
we aren't a part of.

RUSH RANKIN

The Women of Maine

1

Each summer day the sun loosens
you from the last evening's
nervous chill. The polar ice
melting to swell the ocean
another inch this year adds
a mythic dimension to weather
reports: expect rain to spread
acid over the known world.
A Greek steers his ship
into the island he assumed
didn't exist. A heavy drinker,
he heard women calling,
to him, from the sea's mist.

2

The letter you received
includes her longing
and tribute, her gratitude,
so you grin. Her fingered
perfume travels from the far
edge of the continent

to its heart. Her cottage
at night absorbs the wind's
steady pressure. She stands
naked in the darkness
like a secret fact.

3

On the first night she strips
the covers off the bed
even before you return
from the kitchen with a glass
of wine in each hand.
This, in Maine, the damp wood
after a storm, the sea
still churning, the air
a gasp, a thought, absorbed
slowly by the rocks and sand.

4

No wonder women from Maine
stop breathing
a moment when reading
poems to themselves at night
on that far edge
of the continent.

5

You carry her letter
in your satchel
at dusk when mumbling
truisms to yourself
while walking home,
when daylight filters
the glowing mist
of evening around darkening
trees, that terrible aura

of hope, and people suffer
each other's pain.

6

Even so
when she proposes
a fiesta, I picture
her dancing all night
in Maine. I'll fly.
An airplane crosses an abstract
version of the country.
The tinted map I re-fold
after noting the scale
of time to place.

7

In the soothing urgency
of her voice, so smooth
on paper, you feel less aged.
On a rigid bed, alone, she parts
her legs with one hand
to explore, to tease
the stuttering release
of truth, from herself.
Her eyes close inside
the light of the room.

8

Perhaps drinking, the women
of Maine wait in the darkness
in a distant state, in a cottage
on the abrupt coast. She gets up
and stands naked for a moment
in the darkness. She looks out

at the sea she can only hear.
She leans her head for a second
against the pane of glass.
Grey rocks are dimly glowing
on the shore. Her life opens
inside her the sudden shock,
of what? There are ships
in the darkness tilted
against the horizon.

DONALD REVELL

The Hotel Sander

After the storm at sunset
the day's inconsequence
and canal, the heart of it,
is black and white.
Without a superstition
no one is a liar.

When I reached out my arm, my mother was careful, almost
      studious.
She would say, "It is not a piano. It is an alarm."

After the storm, only visible
an aquarium two flights up
in the son's room.
An animal whines.
An automobile brakes.
The fish ride pearls of air in the tank.

To the east of my middle years, I found a pool of water hung
with dragonflies. Stagnant under beautiful skin, the pool, more
closely than a weapon, focussed my attention to the center of

each breath I drew. Erupted a fountain, green on the one hand, green on the other.

The late Dame was his widow.
It is not a negro.
It is a hairpiece.
Without a superstition,
all east surrenders to all west,
the point of travel diminishes to a climax.

When I would touch my face, my mother slapped my hand away. The outline of leaves, missing from the pavement, bears great responsibility for the year ahead, its stone flagon of the truth behind the bookcase, up the hidden stair.

Each to his own veracity
rides a single pearl of air,
miserable parody of a city.
The aquarium upstairs, the storm
murders the truth also.
I was sounding an alarm.

The Other the Wings

Vivid out of nowhere,
the ashen paper-smell of summer
cripples the garden.
The poor peonies
are dead of their own weight,
every wound exposed.

I went walking. In the park, the defunct observatory wore a helmet of hot moonlight. Its basement glowed where the AA meeting, already frantic with cigarette smoke, made exaggerated, weightless gestures like those of astronauts on the lunar surface. Otherness is not the prelude to meaning. The moon cures no addiction, prevents no wars.

Vivid out of nowhere,
the wind is food.
I have my key, I have my penny.
ZumZum, it is 1970,
and I am tired of my dignity.
Nothing in the world sustains it.

On the pavement, jadeweed was an island in its own shadow.
Each house along the street exposed interiors in yellow
lamplight, but no one moved inside. To see things without
imagining their circumstances is the most difficult happiness.
Red hair reaches down to the jadeweed. Summer music begins,
the nowhere passage from lighted house to dark house.

Vivid who were frightened before,
the circumstances of physical life,
weight and wounds,
drift instead of death.
The hairy back of Arnold Schoenberg
is a moth.

I found a wad of paper and picked it up. Inside, intact and
dead, a moth, a brown sex in a white carnation. Things only
fly that have no cause, no allegiances, not even to their bodies.
The effect is catastrophic. I held a naked roof in my hand, a
famished gratitude. Before it died, the moth was not a flower.
It had flown across mountains.

JUDITH ROOT

Small Differences

November light spreads a sheet
behind the trees, shows home
movies of my dreams. My German
relatives rise up like smoke

from burning leaves. Their talk
of altar flowers, deadlines,
the small difference our lives make
floats up to the cloudy shell I watch
for clear light to break through.

Stubborn as old bones, the whole
family is alive and chatting
until I wake and set the memory
straight— Aunt Wilma, Grandma,
dead, Uncle Al, hovering,
a few weeks to live. Aunt Clara,
Dad, blond greying to white,
shadowing into age as imperceptibly
as darkness tarnishes the winter sky
and sleep moves us all into dream.

Naming the Shells

Sand dollars in shallow waves
tumble the light,
drop like small moons
in foam along the shore line.
We fill our pockets, knot
flapping shirttails into sacks.
Stiff as turtles or crabs,
we rasp as we step,
loose sand in the dollars
shifting with stars.

For years we watched commonplace
forecasts fulfill themselves,
a calm surface with scattered
offshore storms, an overcast sky,
a wind that died at dusk.
This pattern, measured daily
by high and low tides,
led us to accept a stingy

claw or clamshell spear
hidden in wet sand. We honed
our expectations to fragments
and ignored the salty spume
that links us like brothers
to the moon.

Now this show, this tumble,
this gift, begs a response.
Naming each shell
after a part of the body,
liver flank tibula,
we make it ours, *femur*
spleen eyelid blood.
Not being medical students
we run out at *heart,*
and since we have stacks
left to name, we call them
one after another: *heart, heart,*
heart, and hear in our voices
the pulse of the tide.

Snail Winter

When the rains came,
snails followed
crossing our bedroom floor
as if they knew the way.
Impudent mollusks.
Wherever they stopped, they stayed,
even one who locked an obscene double-
decker on another's back.
We still pretend they didn't die
inside thin shells
we cracked loose
from the bathroom wall
and dropped

in clattering handfuls
on the pumphouse roof.

We didn't touch them at first,
except to count
the morning's new arrivals
or tease the tentacles
of one too curious
to seal off for sleep.
They seemed to know
their limits.

Never changed direction
to another room
or invaded the tub though it was redwood
like the walls.
But finally there were too many,
too much stalled life
waiting around us.
Who knows
what they had in mind.

An ancient instinct for some shelter
is perhaps the simplest answer,
one which doesn't tease the truth
like claiming they were sent—
eerie messengers—
to wait the winter with us
and line our well.
The water we drank
full
with their sweet decay.

Swallow Creek

I have imagined the stars over Swallow Creek
blinking in the clear-eyed sky.
I have pictured us driving up to the edge
of that mountain, lying on the Land Cruiser's hot hood,
not touching. We would drink whiskey from a bottle
and I would turn toward you,
see your fingers lit red in a cigarette's glow.
I would catch my breath,
tremble there, on the rim
of a new world, and then we would go back
to the campsite. Outside our tent
the fire would burn all night.
You would finger my spine
in the dark, hold my shoulderblades and guide me
into sleep. Our dreams
would curl together.

So you see that I cannot follow you to Swallow Creek.
Instead I will go to Buckhead bars,
wear black spandex pants, thrust my hips
to the music, swaying
as I close my eyes, pretend to feel your fingers
part my lips.
I will chain smoke,
give men a name that is not mine.
I will not think about the things that I might find
there, in the shadow of your own green countryside.

The Swallows of Capistrano

It should not have ended with letters,
with words typed on thick bond

paper. The written word has a finality
I cannot make myself feel.

Last weekend I moved back to our old neighborhood.
I lie awake at night.
From my bed I see a poster
from an old black-and-white movie, *To Have and Have Not.*
If I go into the kitchen I will find a heart-shaped
bottle of vintage port. I am saving
it for you, the sweet red wine that is almost purple,
the true color of blood.

I have been thinking about a gift I gave you,
a hand-blown egg, dyed yellow, painted with flowers.
I told you, *this is to remind you of spring,*
of our constant renewal.

I would like to learn the art of healing.
I would take you to Capistrano, that ruined mission,
the arched stone, the wooded hillside.
I would tell you how the swallows fly by day,
spend their nights in woods and marshes. They always nest in
        pairs,
lay pure white eggs.
They return to Capistrano every year on the same day.
I would take your hand, like this.
We would lie in the grass and wait for the swallows,
knowing full well that their flight is seasonal.

VERN RUTSALA

The Shack Outside Boise

They have brought you here
where a fine brown silt
covers everything. You want

to ask about color
but it is too late.
They have taken that away.
You eat your brown food
with your brown spoon
and talk softly
with your dark cousins, their
bony arms starved thinner
by shadow. You see the sadness
they call possessions,
the helpless objects
they brought here with great effort—
old generators, bald tires,
a trunk full of mildew,
slaughtered mountains
of the broken and useless.
Then slowly in the exhausted light
they divide it up
making sure you get your fair share.

American Dream

I listen hard in the kitchen
Any sound is welcome
The cars go by the late drinkers
The dragass lovers
I listen until one car stops
I look out
It's the old Ford
Trailing vines and garbage
Back from the junkyard
Decorated with dents and rust
Windshield shattered to milk
Cavities where the headlights were
What prodigies of effort
Brought it here
Struggling without gas without tires
But it's back

Terribly risen
Risen and drawn here
Like a dog in a story

Skaters

There are many tonight and the rink
is like a Breughel, such motion
and animation, at first glance
some busy microcosm.

Above the rink I lean on the rail,
my sleeve settling in the residue
of a sticky drink and on the rail
beside it, scratched: *Letitia*

loves Spud. Below, the skaters
circle crazily, looking now like
a swarm but soon you begin
to see that two types stand out:

The helpless scarecrows so tenuous
and bad they command the attention
they fear— you can almost
hear them pray for balance.

The others you notice of course
circle with such skill they seem
to fly. They skate with their hands
behind their backs and show

enormous deference by giving the inept
berths wide enough for ships.
In truth they're in their element,
a kind of royalty down there

but so good that they're benign.
Like royalty they know they need

the awkward to set them off.
One cuts an elaborate figure

of concern for a fallen child
showing he's not only good on skates
but good at heart. Another averts
what we're meant to believe

is a disaster with arms thrown up
and a nifty shift when a scarecrow
falls twenty feet away.
                                        Thinking
of Letitia and Spud who were moved

to pledge their love right here, I realize
the Breughel swirl below just may be
a little version of the world though
all the gestures seem too large,

like a silent movie— mimed
danger and concern, pratfalls,
the rubber-kneed drunks, bad
music in the background,

and love pledged in the balcony.

JEANNINE SAVARD

The Daughter's Brooch

Just before their divorce, still living
Like a king, he bought me a donkey
Pulling a cartload of flowers. The one gold wheel
Under my fingers spun around in the light.
I wanted his drunkenness,
His laughter lost in smoker's cough, his lies

About Lila and Nadine, the secret phone calls
To stop. If I spun and wished, sang
And danced backwards, could he be
An ordinary man? My father with the good sense
Of other fathers, the straight walk forward,
Clear eyes from the dream itself. I waited for years
For him to become the simple man,
The one who'd work days in the shop,
Planing and fitting, windows and doors.
I let him off
The hook, the one that says you tell
The truth. And I was afraid to ask
Was it you or one of your blonde extras
Who saw first the donkey pulling the burden,
The lilacs along the cashmere coast
Of my breast.

The Fall

The gold-flaked plaster body
Hung by one arm from the cross
Above the bottles of pink and red polish.
Beside the solvent in the middle
Of the girl's vanity,
There was a pond with inch-high skaters,
Snow clinging to their skirts and
To the edges where pine cones were placed.
She wondered, looking down into the oval glass,
What the pretty girls would do
If this Christ were to drop
Into their midst on a sunny afternoon
In December. Would they carry it
In their arms to a warm room,
Cover its body with their scarves
Or ask that it be nailed back up
Where it belonged,
Where for years he and the wall
Were one. There was no telling,

Not even about the skater who pretended
To be blind, holding on to the scarf
In front of her, keeping her own body
From falling too far behind the great curve
Of time. She'll never even admit
To the accident of no weather,
A sky without clouds or birds. It is
A world that cannot sustain
The breakable weight of a known god.

A Carnival Figure of Guatemalan Clay

The Devil's on his bike, lead shoes
And wings corrugated
With bone like an accordion.
You can hear him singing
Up-street, he's put on his horns
To make you laugh. He's not
Laughing with you. You don't care,
You're just relieved to see
Movement come on this still
Desert afternoon. You begin
To wonder if everyone else is hiding,
If they somehow, forewarned,
Do not look— not, as when an atom bomb's
Exploding: blindness and worse.
You make a sign like an O
For fear to pass through— a crash
Outside, a goat shot in the trash.

The Descent of Fire

A long window stretches her face
Against the city sky. She's running
In her see-through down the dark
Iron fire escape. Her lover throws caviar
And ice shavings through the grillwork

To the street. Neighbors have been zeroed out
With a cut from the old Hendrix love album.
The woman's burning in the unpardonable
Night: anger pulling at her like a child's
Foot stomping for something more. A stranger's
Laughter angles into a red sky. She reveals
Her breast to a one-eyed dog in the trash
Who's come up with a ham bone surrounded
By the cuttings of her own hair.
The rust and dripping water, lettuce
And outer cabbage leaves under the restaurant's
Spigot are for her the earth . . .
She rubs a finger along the brick wall,
Along her lips and makes a cosmetic with it
To her throat, asks her guardian, her phantom
For a silence, just a silence, without hope.

LAURIE SCHORR

Amusement

Yolanda and I step into the seat:
it swings, back and forth,

before we can fasten any belt.
I hold my breath, grip the bar,
twist the skin of my hands
over it.

A man helps us close the car.
A bolt slams into place,
we rock gently.
He leans closer, smiling.
His lips whisper words
I cannot hear. But Yolanda
looks into the space

between her breasts, which swell
on either side like small mountains.
Sweat glistens through the down
on her upper lip.
Then the man is lost

to motion, as we whip smoothly at
and then past the crowd.
I turn to her, to laugh,
to scream. Her eyes are tearing.
"Men are such bastards," she says,
but her words are lost
to the wind we create.

EVE SHELNUTT

Memory

She plucks a harp, ascends a stair,
I brush her children's satin hair.
Tendrils of a still-born twin
grow like grass, glow like fire.
Trees of harp-string bar the door.

Family

The sun has left the middle of the sky,
the earth is turning swamp.
My father changes wives, my mother men
who live with us; we multiply.
At night we keep the lights off in the hall;
we dream in pairs:
who tends the dove, who sends it out?

The Triumph of Children

That man who came down the street
with his brace of women was our father
long before his taming. Who did it
is dead, the marl of their love
forgotten, closeness without intimacy
slippery with our schemes to get out.
Once she tried to rise, to braid our
hair, her earrings icy on our cheeks.
At table we sat with him like cows
half out of a dream or dreamers waking
on their heels. It was the season of
imagination, but not defective. We
let him go. We even tied his shoes.
The whole city seemed to sway like a
cornfield: his Lovelies, and every
romantic aspect of nature. She would
not want to join him looking like that.
Even now, when some figure breaks into
fantasy, I want to translate, to feel
the familiar take on all mystery
in the evening promenade of young men.

At the Mass Graveyard

The dead have no doubt
that something overwhelming
has happened. They disclose
a sort of detachment,
consuming oblivion.
If they talk,
surely it is of weight:
leaves, moss, myrtle,
white violets, stones.
To carve a branch
breaking over stone

is to lighten them,
yet, for us, the branch
is endlessly breaking.
There is no wretchedness
like flogged men,
but why speak of wounds?
The dead wear no stigmata.
In this whole plain
there is no blood,
only our memories
of their discarded arms,
the train's rumbling,
each like the tooth
of a rake. Here and there
a child is held up
to the narrow opening,
a little blue enamel mug
dancing with every jolt.

O Hero

His was a house in which the father drank.
So the boy came to have a claim over peaches,
not merely those falling bruised and ready
from trees planted at his birth
but over all the wine not yet made
in tomorrow's buzzing,
the knotted cry. Sunlight

at certain hours inflates the downy breasts
of peaches, some orchards from a distance
appear as mounds of children
bored with the game of death.
Patience lies fallow at harvest;
sweet vapors rise from the pickers' bodies
dense with heat. No matter how much they eat
baskets overflow, juice running between wire slats

as though in expiation, without anger,
love. The pits are mute, dazed by light
or a smile of joy. In winter

what then, when the dead draw into anguish
and the living think only of money, masking
their loneliness, what then? He turned away
from this friendly curiosity. And we,
who could find no other outlet for our energy,
waited by the fire, studying our suspect hands.

GEORGIA SINE

Tornado Warning

It was his Mid-Western sensibilities which first
attracted her. The way he had learned from his father
to head for the basement at the first signs of yellow sky
or high winds. He'd wait—playing checkers or reading
old *National Geographics*—listening to the portable
until the tornado passed through or touched down.

She knows that they should not be on the porch
wrapped in blankets watching the sky turn yellow,
the wind blowing their hair wild. It might be safer
to enter the house, wait patiently through the weather
service warnings. When the storm had passed
she could leave, drive home, cook dinner. But she knows
she should leave, risk the drive, the wind, the debris.

She waits for his recognition of the warnings,
feeling like Tantalus tied into a pool
somewhere at the outskirts of Kansas,
wishing that the gods would turn their heads
just once— let her sip the water,
taste the pears and pomegranates.

JOHN SKOYLES

Good Cheer

My mother called all street vendors
by one name: the little men.
And preferred stopping there
to Woolworth's or Schrafft's.
"How about some chestnuts from the little man?"
she'd say, after a gruesome round
through holiday crowds at Macy's.
That phrase first struck me odd
ten years after I heard it:
my father in the hospital,
I came home from college
to comfort my mother.
After one visit, when we left
in early evening, and limousines
and sports cars from New Jersey
headed toward the East Side bars,
she said, "Should we go home, or stop
for something from the little man?"
I loved her for bringing back
that old routine, freshly heard,
just as we verged on permanent change.
I worried so much about my father's heart,
my mother's false good cheer,
that every commonplace seemed significant,
and every significance, absurd.
We stood under a loud umbrella
signed Sabrett's in a whirling script
and I ordered.
It was the first time, too, I really looked
at my mother: all smiles
in a full-length fake-fur coat
with a real fur collar.
And myself: the jacket and tie
chosen for a style

imitating the Ivy League.
The little man, pleased to serve us,
made a serious production
above the mustard well,
and with a delicate flourish
snapped the tissue from the straw.
Then we returned to our apartment
in Queens, to a street
where women always seemed to be sweeping,
and no one shook
when glass and metal crashed,
as if they expected it.

The Head of Tasso

Three sisters lived downstairs,
Anne, Florence and Sarah,
all in their eighties,
each of them ill for weeks at a time,
and when Florence died
I wrote a note of sympathy,
a recollection of the worried grace
with which she stalked
our building's strangers through the stairwells
and tailed the elusive landlord
with a thesis of complaint.
In her will I received
a woodcut of the head of Tasso,
a fiery print her sisters said
any museum would be happy to have.
My books said Tasso took a blow
to the head and after whirled
the streets in insane fits,
but I hung the portrait.
Its afflicted face,
like a horse's suddenly

pulled to a halt,
looked out the window
at a fire escape burglars used,
the news of which
shook the remaining sisters,
who disappeared almost overnight
as if ascending
through a single sleeve of sunlight.
Fastidious, kind, with a roving paranoia
that plowed blood through their veins,
they used to stand in their foyer
of fake roses, tearing petals
to place beneath the bouquets
so they appeared to have dropped there,
once alive.

In Memoriam

We stayed in a resort town that Easter
and walked the beach at low tide,
eyeing what was left behind.
I was with a woman
whose mother had just died.
She seemed less a daughter than a souvenir,
a keepsake bringing back
a familiar "Remember that?"

The motel recalled my room as a boy
where a dog slept beneath the bed.
Driftwood twisted on the walls;
we put out cigarettes
in an ashtray made of shell.

She kept thinking about the past
while I couldn't help
imagining her years later,
as you run into childhood friends,

and the rings of their parents
appear on their hands.

At night I read late,
listening to the waves outside.
The rising and falling was punctual,
obsessed, like the routine
of someone about to break down.
She slept a lot, said little,
and imitated, I thought,
some gestures of her mother.

I never felt like a man there,
and before turning out the light,
I left a glass of water
beside the bed,
as if it had been brought there
in the middle of the night.

DAVE SMITH

The Fisherman's Whore

Like gentle swells
of corn rows that will not fade
from a golf course fairway,
or old burial mounds,
dead boats in low silhouettes

rise from a sweat,
from black marsh mud-beaded where
the town's trash leaches in
bright water-blisters.
Our fathers' worn whores wait.

Along the swing-laden
porches of whitewashed houses you

can hear the lacy swamp grass
hiss angrily, bladed
now in winter's first wind.

Rattling their throats
old fishermen come to sag against
the caved-in ones once more,
all gray as the lies
they scatter to the tides.

Mother-of-pearl garlands
their flanks. Scales, seaworm skins,
shells flash sun like jewels
from womanly curves no
flush of blood freckles darker.

Rust wells steadily out
of pine, yet tight are a few joints.
Passion's hulks, ulcered, too
wear to bear men safely
over thudding seas, still they

hold our unforgotten ways.
Young men come here to find themselves
dreaming, waking, to lie down
in the chines's thighs,
their fathers' fables unbroken.

Today another one goes,
bicycle stacked by a sewered creek,
to chip, to paint, to sing
in love's raw grip
for whatever life offers him.

March Storm, Poquoson, Virginia, 1963

For three days the wind blew northeast,
reeds huddled underwater, bent back and down,

like birds with their heads bowed
in a winged darkness. The tide
held, came on slowly, not impelled
by high slopes to flood and churn
through narrows, but a lapping gray
light mounting the back steps: it came
unnoised, settled among our shoes
at the corners of closets, from
under sofas and rockers licked out
to sweep the rooms free of dust,
socks, dead mice, whatever would swim.

When the sun broke the fourth day's wake
the water retreated in silence,
the oyster boats sank, gentled
in the tops of the pines,
rudders lolling like dog's tongues.
Stunned like drunks gone out
into abrupt noon light, we walked
through the fields, crowded
under the hulls' intimate shadows
to lift up our arms and show proof
of the scarred wounds seen at last
where we had always felt them.
All around us delicate seagrass
uprooted, rose and billowed until
each of us, lean as skeletal fish,
darted off as if to escape
the closing net of oncoming night.

Near the Docks

There was a fire in the night.
Across the street I slept among the others
as the ashes snowed upon small pines.
I slept owning nothing, a child ignorant
of fortune's blistering story, the playful
flash in the dark, the unseen smolder

that would leave us revealed, though
unchanged as the black earth.
I said my prayers for luck
like the man trying to live
in two houses, hoping for time
to leave the old one of his fathers,
its windows with weariness fogged.
The other was half-built, roofless,
green timbers going gray in sun
like a vision that would not be done.

I had climbed there all summer to smoke
after the hours when I would find him
hunched on his wooden stool. Each
morning, halfway between the houses,
on his tongue would be the story
of how they came and of the sea,
his hands weaving wire to a trap,
making careful seams to catch
cunning scuttlers. I saw his wife
already had begun to hang her wash,
its shapes rueful, steaming, ghostly
in sunflare. That day a mongrel
lapped from the ruts of the fire trucks.

I thought little was changed by fire,
only his toolshed limp as a black sail
left in a heap, and that new hole
in the landscape. This was a poor place
where no one came, luckless, desperate,
eternal as guilt. I was the same
as the day before. In silence
I greeted that old one. Now I remember
seeing also, as if for the first time,
the shocking gray face of the sea
was his, fixed, in one quick glance.
It loomed up human and beautiful
as far off the figures of boats
crossed, worked, and seemed to sink
while they burned in the sullen sun.

MARCIA SOUTHWICK

The Ruins

I'd bury my face in my hands but
somebody has to do it,
set the record straight: the combs were hers, the
      razors were his,
and the naked wax doll with the head missing
was mine. I'll step away from the ruins into the sunset.
I'll take a match to the whole thing,
I'll throw it away, the paper.

In the old days, the sun
was stronger,
so full of ambition that it saw through pockets
and blindfolds. No more.
They've taken away birds, they've taken down rafters.
I'm on display, and the sun watches me—
that's wrong,
it's completely self-possessed.

What if I've become one with the rubble?
Do I matter less than splinters of glass?
Do I matter less than spaces where doors used to be?
A button I've lost turns up—
it's here in the ashes, and so are my old gloves.
Why do my hands cast shadows on broken white
      walls?
A last bird cries, making a wild guess.

Here, nothing is private:
The dirt, camouflaged by scorched grass,
shows through in spots like
bare skin on a dead horse's hide.
A few more leaves are absent today,
and everyone knows it.

The Sun Speaks

I search for new meaning
and find black poplars
inaccessible like
locked doors, roses turning brown
from the inside out, and wind
that quickens into an almost material thing
as it nudges aside
a dry leaf here and there
to make room for itself. Shadows
shouldn't clutter the yard, but
they do. On a larger scale,
the landscape is further complicated by
a network of roads and sidewalks.
The entire pattern, seen from a distance, looks
almost life-threatening like
an underground root system. Yet,
on the subject of deserts and naked skin,
I'm still the expert. Who
really belongs here? I don't know. But
if the picket fence surrounding your house
seems less preoccupied than usual
and doesn't hold you in, take a long walk
to see the roses again.
If the night loses track of you,
along with everything else it obliterates:
back yards and sheds, for instance,
slipping out of existence as the night
erases things to perfection, don't worry. I'll be back
to stare down at you from my office of fire.

Horse on the Wall

She deserted you,
the aunt who sang you to sleep.
On your birthday years ago,
she gave you a figurine,

a blue china horse
that broke as you dragged it
across the floor. At five,
you felt the twinge you'd later recognize
as guilt. So here you are,
thirty-three years later,
standing on a street corner,
looking for answers:
It's evening and the first stars
will soon spot you
waving and calling to your friend
who wants to quit writing poetry
but can't. He should have stopped
his car for you.
You hear yourself
call his name again,
and the shock of it is like
the screech of tires rounding a corner.
Maybe you've just called
a name into history,
your voice flying past the great poets,
who lean out of doorways
into the gray rain. Unheard,
a call like that cannot turn back
and loses itself among the vacant
parking lots and side streets.
It's the way your aunt
must have disappeared, leaving you
awake at night, your mind
patching together bits of shadow
into a figure that looked like
a flattened version of the china horse
galloping on the wall.
Maybe your friend,
without a poem in his head,
adjusts the rearview mirror
and sees his own face
staring back at him like a stranger's.

PRIMUS ST. JOHN

Reading a Story to My Child

This is a small boy
In a ragged coat.
Moving through his world
Is a bold paint brush
Briefing on the light in the dark.

In the most subtle way
You are drawn to the heart
Because the heart is the name
Of the story
But you do not know this yet.

He is going to school:
Though you know he must first
Cross the lake,
Whistle to the birds,
And clean out an understanding path
In the tall grass.

He is a good boy
Who adores crows;
He even talks like them.

He is no fool;
He will not hurt you.
He does not talk;
He lives an honest life.

At school, the children
Abhor him.
They see clothes

And the disaster of no voice.
What kind of school is this
That abhors true love?

He may not eat much,
But they are starved.
Boy, you are in the tall grass
And the soil is ruthless.

What do they teach here
That is as nice as our eyes closed?
The school is on a strange page
Farther away than the lines of the smallest trees.
And each parted brush stroke
Is like a squadron of geese.

But the little boy holds on
To his heart.
(Yes Sir) It is better than a bright nickel,
Or a ball,
Or a tall pole.

He does not know
Quite how to write.
He thinks language
Is a series of bizarre pictures.

Though it is loud
It is not sharp like a crow's voice *CAW CAW CAW*.
And it is not bright
Like a birthday of new flowers.
(Yes Sir)
In all of the fields that he knows,
These pictures are not wise—
And he knows this.

At a certain point, there is more
Color on the page

Than in the eyes of a dove
Who is listening.

He looks out of the window—
Home.
Someone there who knows him—
Softly and hard
Sees our storm,
Its ruthlessness
And its subtle tentacles of rain
We have all absorbed.

Hey,
But this is a boy who holds on.
My, you'd want to know this boy.
Now I am on page 8
And afraid for my soul.
At this point I say,
Boy.
(Yes Sir)
I say, Boy
Hold on for us all.

But today, he is given a brush.
He has climbed all the way down
And he has climbed back up
On his strange way that gets here,
And because he is not afraid
Darkness does not hide him.
He knows its crows
And there love is prehistoric

Like shale at the gorge,
Like evening cold,
Like the lonely gills of a fat fish
At the edge of water.

My, My, My,
You'd love this boy

Just for how it feels.

He paints birds at that
Exact moment flight enflames us.
He sees their heads as small prayers
On the lips of the sky.

(*Yes Sir*)
He knows how— this boy;
He knows how their wings are
Soft, ironic smiles that are alive.

My, My, My,
How daddy cries (*Yes Sir*).
This here is just a boy he knows
And won't say why.
A small boy
In a ragged coat.

Carnival

The sun's return is magical;
And once a year, finally
More than we can bear.
That is why, suddenly,
We break out into a sensual
Frenzy of light
And sound
And motion
And color
Plunging ourselves into chaos,
For we are nervous
But we say it is a celebration
As we realize our lives
Have been nothing more
Than a mischief of patterns
And organizations
Against our fear of the capricious—

Like the essence of the trees and caves,
Like the essence of the growing crops,
Like the essence
Of all the herds of animals,
Like the essence of the clan and tribe,
Even our passionate anger,
Even our violence,
Even our cold indifference,
Our clandestine cruelty,
Our gentle warmth,
Our nurturing abundance,
And our generosity
As we struggle with our volatile selves
Trying to become one with the gods.

KIM R. STAFFORD

Walking to the Mailbox

We found a turtle stunned by sunlight
dozing easy with half-shut eyes,
and as I bent down, my little Rosemary,
strapped to my back, stirred and
murmured. When I held its knobbed green
body up, her quick breath moistened
my ear, while the turtle, dazed
by eternity, made perfect unto itself
by so many million years, looked
back at my little one, all wisdom
and danger, trouble and delight
unfurled in the slots of its yellow eyes.

Hunched on the ground again it broke
from its trance, sinewy legs
reaching out, the green skull
of itself tottering slowly away,

made strong by wearing its
own death outward as I did
rising up with Rosemary.

Opening the Book

When our landlord's name was Manlove
and the world was three years old, when
the car wouldn't start and summer was
longer than life and warm with dew
in the soft morning we stepped early
onto the tarred trestle above Tualitin
river water fish nibbled, leaves
flashing between ties Helen counted
for two nephews, who were my brother and me,
and then the parents with the baby between them
singing, *I feel like a morning star.*

On the far side shining grass and dew
we tumbled into the wild orchard deep
with sunlight and spearmint, opened our
blanket to shake out walnuts and bruised
apples, father in the pear calling down
where we were sticky and laughing rolling
late plums into hollows of grass, Helen
pulling down an arc of white roses
so our basket might be filled, mother
humming with bees while my sister slept.

How carefully we walked over the trestle
toward evening, how slow toward winter
and the house that would burn, the strange
changes our bodies would learn and carry
for another sister, for my own child
all our words poured out, and trees
we would hollow into earth and wait
for shade to cover our family
singing *I feel like a morning star.*

Feather Bag, Stick Bag

These five strands bear hair in a split match,
this about seeing two at love kindle my heart.
How much you pay to hear the rest?

This willow stick red thread tied
be that song before Eve wore shame,
before God pluck the garden key out Adam's mouth.
How much you pay to hear it all?

That ship, mother, go down singing.
You hold feather of the bird that saw,
hold feather of the bird that told me
how they all sang when water closed.
You pay me now, I sing it.

Feather bag, stick bag, this little bone
worry me honest about my people
waiting for me pull the skein of that road
all the way out my fist and be done.
They wait, I sing, you pay, that road
ravel me out.

Dust and water, winter road. Feather
bag, stick bag, bone bag all I had
when dust and water been my food.
Not so always. This blue scrap
be ribbon silk, and wrapped inside
she hides, she laughs my song.
Your money jangle out why.

Feather bag, stick bag— see this
penny my anvil hammer pounded flat?
This the song I sing about you
if you don't buy my songs.

Hah! Feather bag, stick bag, bone bag.

WILLIAM STAFFORD

Both Ways

Two things crossed Main Street:
the morning train always telling
its caboose to hurry, or so my father said
when we watched it pass; and
the little unassertive ghost,
that woman my mother told about, falling
all her life past people's windows,
trudging home to that old house
by the river where she starved one winter
and we didn't even notice she was gone.

For Alexis Christa von Hartmann: Proved Not Guilty

It takes awhile, recovering. You confess,
"I think about it. It wasn't true, but what people say
can move in and occupy your mind for awhile.
There are things you can't get rid of just because
        they aren't true."

Years later when the wind comes by where autumn
has piled leaves, you toss them around with a stick.
It is cold and you walk along seeing fields
and a road that enters the great forest. A bird
        flies over.

And there, left alone finally, miles from either home or
destination, you are free. What came by chance
into the middle of your life has diverged again,
and so quietly you didn't know it was gone.

It is now. You are walking. It is evening.

Twelfth Birthday

They never found what slowly descended, silently
disappeared. It was cold that day, breathless
as death and so bright the sycamore levitated
its limbs over the park, afraid of itself, its image
deep in the lake. And whatever it was
descended alone, disappeared not anyone,
maybe was nothing. But the day was real.

And I've never changed.

Preservation

In that new country mountains won't have a name.
Along their slopes a big fence has a sign: "Sorry."
And among those peaks rove the stories
too wild for city people, or too ordinary.

Saved by the wilderness, crowds come around,
more and more like they were. Stars fade;
rivers lose their way. Philosophers try
impossible thoughts, to get back where truth begins.

And a few country people, left when the great change came,
meet in old farmhouses, whispering about those times
when everyone could go where they wanted,
wild without fences around them.

The speakers tremble; their listeners cry out and moan
when they hear the wonderful part— how the earth
was a world once and lay unexplored,
how a mountain was real without any name.

Childhood

I used to lie on my back, imagining
A reverse house on the ceiling of my house
Where I could walk around in empty rooms
All by myself. There was no furniture
Up there, only a glass globe in the floor,
And knee-high barriers at every door.
The low silled windows opened on blue air.
Nothing hung in the closet; even the kitchen
Seemed immaculate, a place for thought.
I liked to walk across the swirling plaster
Into the parts of the house I couldn't see.
The hum from the other house, now my ceiling,
Reached me only faintly. I'd look up
To find my brothers watching old cartoons,
Or my mother vacuuming the ugly carpet.
I'd stare amazed at unmade beds, the clutter,
Shoes, half-dressed dolls, the telephone,
Then return dizzily to my perfect floorplan
Where I never spoke or listened to anyone.

I must have turned down the wrong hall,
Or opened a door that locked shut behind me,
For I live on the ceiling now, not the floor.
This is my house, room after empty room.
How do I ever get back to the real house
Where my sisters spill milk, my father calls,
And I am at the table, eating cereal?
I fill my white rooms with furniture,
Hang curtains over the piercing blue outside.
I lie on my back. I strive to look down.
This ceiling is higher than it used to be,
The floor so far away I can't determine
Which room I'm in, which year, which life.

Shoplifters

I'd smoke in the freezer
among the hooked beefsides,
wondering about the shoplifters
who wept when the manager's
nephew tugged them to his office.
He made me search the women.
I found twenty cans of tuna fish
under the skirt of a mother whose son
drowned in a flash flood out west.
Now he haunted her,
begging for mouthfuls of fish.
Candles fell from a nun's sleeves.
She meant to light the route
for tobogganists on the convent hill.
Two old sisters emptied beans
from their big apron pockets,
claiming they cured rheumatism.
Soon I recognized snow
drifting across faces at the door,
watching in the round mirrors
the way hands snatched out
unhesitatingly at onions.
In the mirrors everyone stole,
buttoning coats again, looking
once over their shoulders
while eggs bulged in a mitten
or salt sifted from their hems.
Did they think me an angel
when I glided in my white uniform
down the soap aisle, preventing
some clutch of fingers?
An old man I caught last year
stuffing baloney down his trousers
lived alone in a dim bedroom.
The manager said cupcake papers
blew across his floor—
hundreds, yellow, white & pink.
Now he peers through the window,

watching me bag groceries
for hours until my hands sweat.

Biography

Perhaps biography is the flat map
Abstracted from the globe of someone's life:
We are interested in the routes and detours.
So I found myself last summer in a storm
Driving down the Main Street of Red Cloud
Looking for Willa Cather's house, which was closed.
Then I drove to the Geographic Center
Of the United States, where she may have once walked
When the red grasses covered the prairie.
I tried to see for a moment through her eyes.
I looked at cows; I turned my head away
From the abandoned motel and two roadside tables—
But it was those forlorn shapes I remembered
Back in my own life, out on the highway.

Sunday Graveyard

"Walks in graveyards
Bore me to death,"
Says the old woman
Walking beside me
Who reads the sunken gravestones
Clucking, clucking—

"Such odd engravings,
A stairway to heaven,
Naked cherubs."
She shakes her head.
Her own stone is smooth,
Paid for, wordless,

"A solid slab
Of grey marble
Thick as a wrist,"
She tells me, pointing—
"No poetry like this."
Just her name

"Elizabeth"
Cut so deep
It won't blur
For two centuries.
"Time enough," she laughs,
"For judgment day."

She calls her husband
Who lags behind us.
She wants her dinner,
Complains of cold.
Half-blinded by cataracts,
She can't read

Fainter inscriptions
Meant to console
Women like herself,
Or warn the ironical
Like me, who think they'll face
Death more honestly.

GERALD STERN

Peddler's Village

The small grey bird that fit inside the hand
of a nine year old girl is himself a grandfather
with a tear stuck to the side of his round face;

but he hopped on the red bricks and absentmindedly
pecked at her hand as if he were still young and blue,
with oily wings and a stomach full of seeds.

If she could see his heart she would know how terrified he was.
She would take off her colored handkerchief and stop being his
    grandmother;
she would take away his paper bed and stop being his sister and
    his bride.

If she knew how old he was she would bow down
and kiss his loose feathers
and listen carefully to his song.

There had to be wisdom with all that age,
something he could give her,
something she could remember him by and love him for;

there had to be some honor, some revelation,
some loveliness before he died;
before the lice robbed him,
before the bitter wire snapped him in two,
before a thousand tragedies took away his warmth and
    happiness.

Nobody Else Living

Nobody else living knows that song as well as I do.
On bad days I fill the tub with hot water
and rest my head on the freezing porcelain.
I fill the courtyard with sounds.
They come through the frosted glass,
they come through the transom. All that wonderful pity,
all that broken bliss, for twenty or thirty minutes
now rich and reminiscent and warm,
now cloudy and haunted.

I Hate My Moaning

I hate my staring. I hate my moaning. Sometimes
I lie there in the morning arguing
against myself. I hold a mirror up
above the telephone so I can snip
a long hair from my eye. I balance a cup
of coffee on my stomach. Sometimes I sing,
sometimes I hold a feather against my nose,
sometimes I prop the clock against my ear,
sometimes I drag the speakers across the floor
and turn the volume up. There is a hole
above my head, the plaster is dropping, the lath
is exposed; there is a blanket over the window;
I hold it up with nails, it tears in the center
and lets a stream of light in; I can tell
when it's six o'clock, and seven o'clock, it is
my hour, the blanket is full of holes, the light
comes through the threads, it is a greyish light,
perfect for either love or bitterness,
no exaggeration or deceit.

JAMES TATE

Teaching the Ape to Write Poems

They didn't have much trouble
teaching the ape to write poems:
first they strapped him into the chair,
then tied the pencil around his hand
(the paper had already been nailed down).
Then Dr. Bluespire leaned over his shoulder
and whispered into his ear:
"You look like a god sitting there.
Why don't you try writing something?"

Deaf Girl Playing

This is where I once saw a deaf girl playing in a field.
Because I did not know how to approach her without startling
her, or how I would explain my presence, I hid. I felt
so disgusting, I might as well have raped the child, a grown
man on his belly in a field watching a deaf girl play.
My suit was stained by the grass and I was an hour late
for dinner. I was forced to discard my suit for lack of
a reasonable explanation to my wife, a hundred dollar suit!
We're not rich people, not at all. So there I was, left
to my wool suit in the heat of summer, soaked through by
noon each day. I was an embarrassment to the entire firm:
it is not good for the morale of the fellow worker to flaunt
one's poverty. After several weeks of crippling tension,
my superior finally called me into his office. Rather than
humiliate myself by telling him the truth, I told him I
would wear whatever damned suit I pleased, a suit of armor
if I fancied. It was the first time I had challenged his
authority. And it was the last. I was dismissed. Given
my pay. On the way home I thought, I'll tell her the truth,
yes, why not! Tell her the simple truth, she'll love me
for it. What a touching story. Well, I didn't. I don't
know what happened, a loss of courage, I suppose. I told
her a mistake I had made had cost the company several
thousand dollars, and that, not only was I dismissed, I
would also somehow have to find the money to repay them
the sum of my error. She wept, she beat me, she accused
me of everything from malice to impotency. I helped her
pack and drove her to the bus station. It was too late to
explain. She would never believe me now. How cold the
house was without her. How silent. Each plate I dropped
was like tearing the very flesh from a living animal. When
all were shattered, I knelt in a corner and tried to imagine
what I would say to her, the girl in the field. What could
I say? No utterance could ever reach her. Like a thief
I move through the velvet darkness, nailing my sign on
tree and fence and billboard. DEAF GIRL PLAYING. It is
having its effect. Listen. In slippers and housecoats
more and more men will leave their sleeping wives' sides:

tac tac tac: DEAF GIRL PLAYING: tac tac tac: another
DEAF GIRL PLAYING. No one speaks of anything but nails
and her amazing linen.

My Great Great Etc. Uncle Patrick Henry

There's a fortune to be made in just about everything
in this country, somebody's father had to invent
everything— baby food, tractors, rat poisoning.
My family's obviously done nothing since the beginning
of time. They invented poverty and bad taste
and getting by and taking it from the boss.
O my mother goes around chewing her nails and
spitting them in a jar: You should be ashamed
of yourself she says, think of your family.
My family I say what have they ever done but
paint by numbers the most absurd disgusting scenes
of plastic squalor and human degradation.
Well then think of your great great etc. Uncle
Patrick Henry.

Contagion

When I drink
I am the only man
in New York City.
There are no lights,
but I am used to that.
There are the staircases
that go forever upward
like the twisted branches

of a cemetery willow.
No one has climbed them
since prohibition.
And the overturned automobiles
stripped to their skeletons,

chewed clean
by the darkness.

Then I see the ember of
a cigarette in an alley,
and know that I am no longer
alone. One of us
is still shaking.
And has led the other
into some huddle of extinction.

Rustin Steel Is Driving the Crew to the River

Rustin Steel is driving the crew to the river. A long
gunmetal Cadillac has stopped in front of him. He tries
the brakes. A little, a little more. He presses the pedal
all the way to the floor: nothing. With both palms he
presses the horn. No sound. Nothing. No horn, no brakes.
He has with him the best crew in twenty years of driving
the crew bus. He pulls the steering wheel right off its
sprocket, and goes flying through the windshield into
the river. He starts paddling toward shore. The crew
is standing on the banks, cheering! Now he straightens
his course and stretches his arms toward Exeter, twenty
miles downstream, his archenemy, his only hope.

ALBERTA TURNER

Anyone, Lifting

Someone's hiding in the graveyard:
police car across the drive, helicopter
above. Dogs are staked.

Someone is hiding here, mint in his sleeves,

full length on a stone, ears flared out.

And something is missing.

They want a man in a crouch, a woman with
hair over her eyes, anyone   lifting.

Elm Street

Houses trot toward us,
some have stars on their foreheads.
They trot porch to porch, screen doors snapping,
shades lowering and lifting.
Just out of reach they toss their eaves,
lower their front steps, and begin to graze.

Meditation Upon Ought

Ought is a Sunday soreness:
A woman has drawn a star with her clothesline,
drawn it from a center pole around a young birch
and out to another and back, five times.

A man has circled his house with used tires
and filled them with topsoil and planted petunias.

Their child has gathered acanthus pods
and strung them the same distance apart
and lowered his stringer into the horse trough.

The aphorist says, "Invent what you want
and you'll have what you ought."
But *ought* is surely rounder and wider than that:
Camels go through, with double humps; and freaks
drop through without even dragging their chins.
Anyone can sit on the rim and fish— real fish.

Lost Child

In the suburbs, the nativity scene:
Mary and Joseph's unremarkable faces gaze
at their infant buried in snow.
The nearby reindeer, out of his story,
can't know
it is his turn to speak, to tell
of Joseph's anonymity,
the abandoned playroom where
except for a few white weeks
he's kept
with these chipped faces, the sentimental
pale lips. But this is
the story of the lost child,
the parents gazing at blankness,
that lumpy erasure.
This is a little display
of powerlessness,
of what can never be done
until time says yes,
until the morning when
the mother lets the dog out
and shovels, at last,
the infinite child
into sight again.

The Debt

A mother shouts for her child Billy.
The shout is like a curse
that has been cracked inside a woman's mouth

a thousand years.
But the child will return for that voice.
It's what he has after all.

The mother calls
and everyone in the building
must shudder a bit,
that voice, that little stick of despair,
making even the oldest remember
how as a child they wondered
why they should bother
to learn a new game.

What if that woman shakes her head
and walks inside
and never calls the boy again?
Or no. Here it comes, that voice
like a debt to the world, a debt
of cold and ugly music   .
necessary for one child.

A Daughter

Water on the white blossoms,
warm, almost like the touch of oil.
To be ridiculous and beautiful was
one task for a daughter.

When she stepped out, at first,
her eyes would not open,
her eyes that hurt her.

I think she was always young like that.
At the camp three boys tussled
while another, dark-haired,
stood apart
watching them with so much joy

that it shamed me,
the peculiar dreamy happiness
of some children.

On the orange earth
little pines,
the flowering trees
that seemed earnest, transparent,
her happiness slowly
beginning as if she were that child
we passed.

And I remember her
stepping out of hell
as it cracked open
just enough to let her go,
dazed, dirt still caking her face.

Now impossible for her to remember.
As if a garden cannot be
itself at night. Once
in a cottage an old man
wound a phonograph and danced for us.
His white chest shook
to the music. It was
as if the past had appeared inside
the room, very near and tired, at last

trickling around us like
the smell of earth, of flowers
that are white only in daylight,
that close to a slender point
the color of ink.

Robert Wallace

A Fresco of Swans and Bears

The moon is a furnace,
sun
a stormy mirror.

Thin vines of smoke
trail
under the starry rafters.

The story always has another
ending.
Night. The salty rose.

Driving By

On August nights,
in little towns you sometimes see
from the throughways
bloom

the ball field lights—
domes
of smoky brilliance:
brighter than daylight colors,

figures through wire-mesh on the green,
figures in the plank stands,
a tiny moon
dropping out toward left.

They stay
much as we left them—
lichen of the blue American nights
from which we come.

Riding in a Stranger's Funeral

It is now 24 years since I rode in a stranger's funeral,
waved into the procession, at a stop light,
by a policeman who mistook my having my headlights on
in the daylight (to spare an overcharging battery).

Then I saw the cars behind with lights on, too,
and little pennants on their fenders,
and I understood. That was in blossomy April
in Lynchburg, and I did not turn off or drop aside

because I feared the cars behind might follow me.
So I went on, trees, shops, dogs, and passersby
on the sidewalks alongside, going about their affairs,
sunshine through the windshield warm on my knees.

And I said to myself that any man justly
might mourn any other, since none can live forever,
and that someday, too, who knew when,
I might ride similarly surprised, but in the lead.

At the natural-stone gateway when, instead of turning,
I drove straight on, my kitetail of cars correctly
turned and followed the other cars following the hearse,
into the cemetery, and in among the trees.

The Double Play

In his sea-lit
distance, the pitcher winding
like a clock about to chime comes down with

the ball, hit
sharply, under the artificial
banks of arc lights, bounds like a vanishing string

over the green

to the shortstop magically
scoops to his right whirling above his invisible

shadows
in the dust redirects
its flight to the running poised second baseman

pirouettes
leaping, above the slide, to throw
from mid-air, across the colored tightened interval,

to the leaning-
out first baseman ends the dance
drawing it disappearing into his long brown glove

stretches. What
is too swift for deception
is final, lost, among the loosened figures

jogging off the field
(the pitcher walks), casual
in the space where the poem has happened.

In a Spring Still Not Written Of

This morning
with a class of girls outdoors, I saw
how frail poems are
in a world burning up with flowers,
in which, overhead,
the great elms
—green, and tall—
stood carrying leaves in their arms.

The girls listened equally
to my drone, reading, and to the bees'
richocheting
among them for the blossom on the bone,

or gazed off at a distant mower's
astronomies of green
and clover, flashing,
threshing in the new, untarnished sunlight.

And all the while, dwindling,
tinier, the voices—Yeats, Marvell, Donne—
sank drowning
in a spring still not written of,
as only the sky
clear above the brick bell-tower
—blue, and white—
was shifting toward the hour.

Calm, indifferent, cross-legged
or on elbows half-lying in the grass—
how should the great dead
tell them of dying?
They may come to time for poems at last,
when they have found they are no more
the beautiful and young
all poems are for.

Michael Waters

Keats' Lips

1

   In the death mask by Gherardi,
  the flesh has already fled
the formal bones of the face,
   chiseled cheek and belled brow,

   but the lips remain swollen,
  almost pursed, what's left

of Keats' tumultuous spirit
          struggling to forsake the mouth.

          Keats might have been his own
     best poem, transmutable as smoke,
but his lips were impassable:
          "I lifted him up in my arms,"

               Severn wrote, "and the phlegm
          seemed boiling in this throat."
And when the body was no more
     than a flask, the last vial

          of blood broken in his lungs,
     the sticks of foreign furniture,
encrusted linens and nightshirt,
          even the door and window-frame

          were taken by the police
     and set aflame in the piazza
below the barren, February steps,
     Bernini's marble boat

          showering the air, bearing
     the antique smell of Keats'
earthly possessions toward the sea
          in the slow swirl of its grain.

2

               His death mask lies in glass,
          facing a sky the color of straw.
The fireplace in his room is shut.
          Tourists throng the square

               when the steep steps flower
          and the light veers violet,

sift maps in Babington's Tea Room
        and loiter below Keats' window.

        In the hotel that night we argued,
    hurt each other with words,
then made love, that blind, desperate
        lovemaking born of loneliness.

        Let me tell you this—
    when her face flushed with orgasm,
as she briefly lost all control,
        I was praying for Keats, his lips,

        the language touched with fever
    that bears us away from our bodies
and soothes the bruised soul,
        if only for a few moments.

        We rose with the clamor
    of street cleaners and vendors
fronting fruit stands and flower stalls,
        to find the sun still cloaked

        with smoke rising off the Tiber.
    Keats loved the light on his face
when he paused on the promenade,
        and gathered momentary faith

        when the hundred gray pigeons
    began their awkward, flapping ascent
toward the gables and red tiles,
        then vanished above the rooftops.

Miles Weeping

To hear Miles weep
    for the first time, the notes bent
        back into his spent frame to keep

them from soaring away—
I had to click the phonograph off
    and hug myself to stop the shaking.
        I'd recognized a human cry
    beyond any longing given a name.
If ever he let go that grief
    he might not touch his horn again.
        That cry rose in another country,
    full-throated in awkward English.
I still have the envelope, unstamped,
    addressed to "Mother/Father," its oily
        scrap of paper torn from a primer,
    the characters like the inky
root-hairs scrawling the washed-out soil.
        Lek—every boy's nickname—
            wrote he was "to be up against,"
    meaning, I guess, that his future
was end-stopped, one unbroken line
    of tabletops waiting to be wiped.
        He'd walked miles along the coast
    to find us combing the beach, then
stood, little Buddhist, with bowed head
    while we read his letter, composed
        with the help of the schoolmaster.
    How could we deny the yearning
ambition to abandon the impossible
    land of his fathers, to begin again?
        We could only refuse in a silent way.
    When someone asked Miles Davis
why he wouldn't play ballads anymore,
    he replied, "Because I love them too much."
        All that we never say to each other.
    The intimacies we can't complete.
Those ineluctable fragments. To be up against.

Koh Samui
Thailand

The Mystery of the Caves

I don't remember the name of the story,
but the hero, a boy, was lost,
wandering a labyrinth of caverns
filling stratum by stratum with water.

I was wondering what might happen:
would he float upward toward light?
Or would he somersault forever
in an underground black river?

I couldn't stop reading the book
because I had to know the answer,
because my mother was leaving again—
the lid of the trunk thrown open,

blouses torn from their hangers,
the crazy shouting among rooms.
The boy found it impossible to see
which passage led to safety.

One yellow finger of flame
wavered on his last match.
There was a blur of perfume—
mother breaking miniature bottles,

then my father gripping her,
but too tightly, by both arms.
The boy wasn't able to breathe.
I think he wanted me to help,

but I was small, and it was late.
And my mother was sobbing now,
no longer cursing her life,
repeating my father's name

among bright islands of skirts
circling the rim of the bed.
I can't recall the whole story,
what happened at the end . . .

Sometimes I worry that the boy
is still searching below the earth
for a thin pencil of light,
that I can almost hear him

through great volumes of water,
through centuries of stone,
crying my name among blind fish,
wanting so much to come home.

DARA WIER

The Innate Deception of Unspoiled Beauty

My silk legs give rise to bird calls
removing all evidence of my wish:

that those moments which the brain contrives
first to link, then to pull apart will find each

its place to settle, sink, sufficient while it turns
the scale toward no particular point.

Rather right on through may they desist
bedrock and proscribe their own boundaries;

some to forsake me, others to state their claims
near those places in which birds knit

nests of grass fiber and fall prey to nothing
save their most natural enemies.

Lucille's Kumquat Colored Kimono

lies on her chest of drawers,
highboy
dusty with baby powder,
pins,
hairballs rolling across
veneer.

This morning the bedroom
steams.

On the neck of her dress
Ernie's sweat,
not quite the color
of her kimono, dries
like pork drippings.

Everything is wet.

Damp enough to warp.

Her face
hot as a jimmied lock
keeps kissing him,
moving his mouth.

Every wrinkle shows.

Ernie goes on to work,
Lucille bends low,
ironing nuisance out.

Barely There

It isn't fair is another way
to say it isn't pretty,

a slighter way of saying
beauty's flown the coop,

gone away where
beauty's merely an idea.

The cardinal in the bare
bridal wreath registers.

The golden fish, lit up,
on top the church registers.

The elastic play of light
over the river's current

registers. Lobelia's blue
shock at sunset,

the boy and girl lost
in dolls and blocks

register. Here's a mechanical
genius, sentient and lost.

I hear the new Buddhist
coming by his voice

and lackadaisical drum's thump
from a long, long way off.

Lucille and Ernie's Master Bedroom

In the closet
dolorous madonnas
taped to the wall
in chorus rows,
ladies in waiting

disguised as angels
stirring in prayer.

Rich, the hand which
passes in blessing this.
Quiet enough for wool carpets,
lit cigarettes, linen bedding,
gold gilded eyelids, lashes,
sequins, Amens.

Daytrip to Paradox

Just as you'd expect
my preparations were painstaking
and exact. I took two

butane lighters and a cooler
of ice. I knew the route
had been so well-traveled

there'd be a store for necessities
and tobacco and liquor and axes.
And near the Utopian village of Nucla

three Golden Eagles watched me
from a salt cedar tree. One of them
held its third talon hard in the eye

of a white Northern Hare. Audubon
couldn't have pictured it better.
Everything was perfect. Naturally

it made me think of Siberia,
the bright inspirational star
that's handed down the generations,

and the long, terrible nights
of the pioneers' journey to paradise.
The valley on the way to Paradox

             was flat, there would be no choice,
nothing to get me lost.
             Cattleguards, gates and fencing

bordered the open range. Of course
      I crossed a narrow bridge
             to get into Paradox proper.

      In the store that doubled
as town hall and post office
             there was an account book for everybody

laid square on the counter.
      No one was expected to pay
             hard cold cash in Paradox apparently.

RENATE WOOD

Blood

That day they had slaughtered on the farm,
and a woman came up the road toward the house
with a bucket of fresh blood.
It was war time. We couldn't pay for meat,
but blood was cheap. And with each step
it sloshed from side to side below the white
enameled rim, churning a ring of pale pink bubbles.
We measured salt and spices and watched
the red broth simmering. On the wiped kitchen table
we sliced the loaves of bread and dipped
the porous slabs into the broth now cooling
in our midst. Some of the children screamed
and wouldn't touch it with their finger tips
where, when we dipped the bread, the broth
etched dark red scythes under our nails.
The greased sheets filled with soggy slabs,

we baked the bread till it was toasted:
more brown than red, it tasted of spiced broth.
Some of us wouldn't eat because of its color
or smell or because we couldn't forget
the bucket like a deep, round wound.
But those who did ate all, a whole bucket
soaked into bread, now soaking inside us.
And we thought how this morning the blood
had flowed inside the cow, how it flowed
in all the cattle on that farm, in the horses,
the rabbits, the mice, the birds, and in us.
And we, the farm, the town and towns across all borders
became a pool, a lake, a sea of blood,
one big flood, one single pulse beating,
drumming one syllable over and over again,
and we didn't know, though we kept listening,
whether it was life drumming inside us or death.

The Pilot

Face down on the sled,
limbs sagging into the snow,
he was huge— like an old spruce
after it's been felled, no longer
foreshortened by our upward glance.
We hadn't known a man looks bigger
when he's dead. This was not
the enemy we'd seen above us after school
soaring across the valley
no bigger than a pencil sharpener,
this was a man— torn overalls,
a birthmark on his neck.
If only he could see us now from above,
that circle surrounding the sled
like filings neatly arranged
around a magnet's length: kids
staring with squeamish stomachs
smaller than his fist, nuns with flapping gowns,

nervous wings against his stillness,
teenagers with swastikas
on their skinny arms and those old men—
mere dwarfs compared to him.
He lay there so quietly, as though
not to scare us, to keep
the order of the field intact, and yet we knew
that he was frozen there in place, as frozen
as that bloody rose below his mouth in the snow,
while the small puffs of our breath
steamed up and fused, looming
briefly, but larger than he, in the air.

Cabbages

I can no longer talk to cabbages
the way I did when I was ten, but still
each time I cut through cupped leaves
into the heart, I hesitate. When I was ten,
for months, on my way home from school,
I stopped at the glass case of photographs
where a girl dressed in white
lay in an open casket hung with vines.
My mother said it was distasteful,
such pictures of the dead.
My sister's photograph was taken
laughing and waving to us from a sleigh.
After the funeral I buried her doll
in the cabbage bed. I knew my sister was watching
from the rocking chair by her window,
her white-blond hair bobbing
with the motion of the white butterflies
that bounced from cabbage head to cabbage head.

From that day on the cabbages
were my witnesses. At night under the full moon
I could see them from my window,
an assembly of skulls

that had pushed through the ground
for a breath of air. Then I understood:
the dead demand attention, expect to feed
on your loneliness, your games, your rituals.
My sister wanted to hear herself
in my voice, use my hands
to pick the caterpillars from the outer leaves,
and when she tired, sleep
inside the white layers of the heart.

C. D. WRIGHT

Scratch Music

How many threads have I broken with my teeth. How many
times have I looked at the stars and felt ill. Time here is divided
into before and since your shuttering in 1978. I remember
hanging onto the hood of the big-fendered Olds with a mess of
money in my purse. Call that romance. Some memory precedes
you: when I wanted lederhosen because I'd read *Heidi*. And how
I wanted my folks to build a fall-out shelter so I could arrange
the cans. And coveting mother's muskrat. I remember college.
And being in Vista: I asked the librarian in Banks, the state's
tomato capitol, if she had any black literature and she said they
used to have *Lil Black Sambo* but the white children tore out
pages and wrote ugly words inside. Someone said if I didn't like
Banks I should go to Moscow. I said, Come on, let's go outside
and shoot the hoop. I've got a jones to beat your butt. I haven't
changed. Now if I think of the earth's origins, I get vertigo.
When I think of its death, I fall. I've picked up a few things. I
know if you want songbirds, plant berry trees. If you don't want
birds, buy a rubber snake. I remember that town with the Alcoa
plant I toured. The manager kept referring to the workers as
Alcoans. I thought of hundreds of flexible metal beings bent
over assemblages. They sparked. What would I do in Moscow.
I have these dreams— relatives loom over my bed. We should
put her to sleep Lonnie says. Go home old girl, go home, my

aunt says. Why should I go home before her I want to say. But I am bereft. So how is Life in The Other World. Do you get the news. Are you allowed a pet. But I wanted to show you how I've grown, what I know: I keep my bees far from the stable, they can't stand how horses smell. And I know sooner or later an old house will need a new roof. And more than six years have whistled by since you blew your heart out like the porchlight. Reason and meaning don't step into another lit spot like a well-meaning stranger with a hat. And mother's mother who has lived in the same house ten times six years, told me, We didn't know we had termites until they swarmed. Then we had to pull up the whole floor. 'Too late, no more . . .,' you know the poem. But you, you bastard. You picked up a gun in winter as if it were a hat and you were leaving a restaurant: full, weary, and thankful to be spending the evening with no one.

The Lesson

This is the chair. This is the lamp. Here is your pencil. The switch is over there. That book lives in the drawer. You speak well. The mirror doesn't work. Those bracelets belonged to a former guest. She had two children she saw only once in a while. Then she wore shadow and silver. Your bed is good and hard. The fruit is cool and dark. People are friendly here. The barman has information to burn. If the moon becomes too much you can close this gown. From the gallery you see the big lights of our Holy Father's summer place, and the flower farms. The lake turns purple from the fertilizer. It is so lovely, it is a pity the fish have to go belly up. The other woman kept a boa for a pet. When her children came she would glisten and alternately glow. Leave your soiled things where you will. Service is complete. You enjoy typing. I can tell. If you wake up bleeding from the mouth, use the spider's web as a stypic. Would your hair be red everywhere. She was what you call a bottle blond. Not a true blond. In the beginning, she was fervent, more fervent, most fervent. Try staying in the vocative case. That window has been painted shut. The radio is for your listening and dancing pleasure. Do you cotton to Dixieland. Excuse my little joke. You will have to share a toilet with a man

who plucks his eyebrows. Allow me. Please, that is very heavy.
Let me. Would you like to make a long distance telephone call.
Do you rent a safety deposit box also. You see we are very
modernaire. Did you observe as you came in, the Monument to
Tomorrow. Is this the first time you are having your face peeled.

Hotels

In the semi-dark we take everything off,
love standing, inaudible; then we crawl into bed.
You sleep with your head balled up in its dreams,
I get up and sit in the chair with a warm beer,
the lamp off. Looking down on a forested town
in a snowfall I feel like a novel—dense
and vivid, uncertain of the end—watching
the bundled outlines of another woman another man
hurrying toward the theater's blue tubes of light.

This Couple

Now is when we love to sit before mirrors
with a dark beer or hand out leaflets
at chainlink gates or come together after work
listening to each other's hard day. The engine dies,
no one hurries to go in. We might
walk around in the yard not making a plan.
The freeway is heard but there's no stopping
progress, and the week has barely begun. Then
we are dressed. It rains. Our heads rest
against the elevator wall inhaling a stranger;
we think of cliffs we went off
with our laughing friends. The faces
we put our lips to. Our wonderful sex
under whatever we wear. And of the car
burning on the side of the highway. Of jukeboxes
we fed. Quarters circulating with our prints.
Things we sent away for. Long drives. The rain. Cafes

where we ate late and once only. Eyes of an animal
in the headlamps. The guestbooks that verify
our whereabouts. Your apple core in the ashtray.
The pay toilets where we sat without paper. Rain.
Articles left with former lovers. The famous
ravine of childhood. Movie lines we've stood in
when it really came down. Moments
we have felt forsaken: waiting for the others
to step from the wrought iron compartment,
or passing through some town with the dial
on a Mexican station, wondering for the life of us,
where are we going and when would we meet.

One Summer

Not even Goldie could have told
—with her talent for telling—
I would sit here at the end
of the wild broom in my wrinkled linen,
Lives of the Artists on my knees,
a window open on flowering tobacco fields
and the ancient Antolini farmhouse;
she could not have pictured me
so peaceable and sound,
defecating merrily under the wheeze
of Arnoldo's accordian
against the whick of Mita's deft sickle.

FRANZ WRIGHT

The Needle: For a Friend Who Disappeared

Just one more time. Only one—
the small rose of blood blooming in the syringe—
one to compel haunted speech to the lips,

sure. Some immense seconds pass. Dusk's
prow slowly glides right up Avenue B;
the young Schumann's two personalities
continue discussing each other
in the diary. Your eyes
move to the warning
on a pack of cigarettes—
good thing you're not pregnant!
Still no speech, but no pain either,
no New York,
nothing,
sweet.
You happen to know that you're home.
And how simple it was, and how smart
to come back: in the moon
on its oak branch
the owl slowly opens
its eyes like a just severed head
that hears its name called out,
and spreads its wings
and disappears;
and the moth leaves the print
of its lips on the glass, lights
on the lamp's stillwarm bulb,
the napper's forehead,
his hand, where it rests
down the chair arm,
fingers
slowly opening.

Pawtucket Postcards

Neon sign missing a letter

Firearm with an obliterated serial number

There's always death
But getting there—

you can't just say the word

Rhode Island Artificial Lumb Co.

Lights of the abandoned
households reflected
in the little river through the leaves

The posthistoric clouds

Joseph Come Back As the Dusk (1950 - 1982)

The house is cold. It's raining,
getting dark. That's Joseph

for you: it's that time
of the day again.

We had been drinking, oddly enough.
He left.

I thought, a walk—
It's lovely to walk.

His book and glasses on the kitchen table.

Entry in an Unknown Hand

And still nothing happens. I am not arrested.
By some inexplicable oversight

nobody jeers when I walk down the street.

I have been allowed to go on living in this
room. I am not asked to explain my presence
anywhere.

What posthypnotic suggestions were made; and

are any left unexecuted?

Why am I so distressed at the thought of taking
certain jobs?

They are absolutely shameless at the bank—
you'd think my name meant nothing to them. Non-
chalantly they hand me the sum I've requested,

but I know them. It's like this everywhere—

they think they are going to surprise me: I,
who do nothing but wait.

Once I answered the phone and the caller hung up—
very clever.

They think that they can scare me.

I am always scared.

And how much courage it requires to get up in the
morning and dress yourself. Nobody congratulates
you!

At no point in the day may I fall to my knees and
refuse to go on, it's not done.

I go on

dodging cars that jump the curb to crush my hip,

accompanied by abrupt bursts of black-and-white
laughter and applause,

past a million unlighted windows, peered out at
by the retired and their aged attack-dogs—

toward my place,

the one at the end of the counter,

the scalpel on the napkin.

KAREN ZEALAND

Passion at the Chat 'n Chew Diner

She was untouched by lust, which they might
have forgiven. Except for her attitude; the way
she minced across the diner's dirty linoleum
as if innately suspicious of anything sticky.
A perpetual country station plied desire;
Amelia immune. Even dead,

what a country boy deplores is being
ignored. They plotted revenge. Half a dozen
in a booth, playing 7-card stud.
No tattoos, they said; no truckers. Their pawn

of destiny, arriving at the Chat 'n Chew in a dusty
Chevy. Balding, a corpulent salesman of hygiene
products; a receipt pad in his glove compartment
for jotting down sentiments. Amelia, won
by a four-line ditty.

The romance progressed until a dream
Amelia had. A Thanksgiving turkey
big as a dinosaur. Huge, meaty
thighs. An ocean of drippings.
Unnerved to the trussed cones
of her bosom, Amelia ended
it with Albert.

She continued through her days, eyes glazed
as a plate of eggs, shushing customers

for Tammy Wynette and the Statler Brothers.
Nothing she could tell herself, but knew.
The pain pristine. The delicious gift
of loss. Half heard beneath the words,
in the pauses
of a country-western song.

A Still Life, Untitled

Three limbs from the same stem of a winter
lilac. The angles they cut
in our dining room window. A cylinder
suspended in air. The pattern in stone
on the wall of our neighbor's house.
Beyond it sky,
underlined with mountains, the curve of trees.
Simple.
Until I try to say the layers
of bark in the lilac. How they are revealed.
What I know of wind in this empty
feeder. How the rooftops, the trees drop
from the wall's hard edge. How lies
I would tell you I can't
in the presence of these stones.

The Primitives Knew How Defenseless

they were. Without convenience
stores or an ambulance. That's why
they built altars, offered fruit,
some poor unfortunate's

virgin daughter. My own
sent off by Security's Fool
without a warning. Her throat closed,
face inflated like a fish dead

for days in water. By lobster,
they note on the med-alert
bracelet I fasten to her
like an amulet.

LISA ZEIDNER

Transvestite

How easy to tell it's a man,
though the gestures are feminine.
Popeye jawline and hands
scaled too large—coltish,
as if he simply hasn't finished
growing into his gender—clash
with red heels and wafty dress.

The overkill of sexual semaphore
is a dead giveaway,
as the nouveau riche in their fur,
jewels and chauffeured limousines
bespeak insecurity, not luxury,
but then whores also dress whorishly,
hence the doubletake:

maybe just a squarish, gaudy woman?
No. Behind him at line
for tickets at the train station,
I smell something indescribably male
that turns the perfume petrochemical.
The smell is animal, hormonal,
more real and subtle than the way

hairy legs, hairy chests and baritones
leak through to blow the drag cover
of wolves in sheep's clothing

in old movies like "Some Like It Hot."
To think this whole masquerade
only serves to attract other men— why not,
in this day and age, simply be gay?

Because nothing is simple, especially sex,
though maybe not for most quite this complex:
a comedy of errors in which a boy actor
dresses up as a girl who dresses up as a boy,
except at the end of the play
order is restored, "and so to bed"
with the destined mate,

whereas in real life all the world's a stage
or a train station— entrances, exits,
nothing permanent except the state of flux,
the lockers at the train station
monopolized by the homeless who enjoy here
if not camouflage, at least a little peace.
The travelers keep their distance,

stare obliquely, as they do at the transvestite.
Staring myself, I think of dead oppossums
on the highway, of civilization's savagery,
wishing the poor guy could be
in a jungle somewhere, tall
and fit, naked except for a single,
simple loincloth.

Bach

My birth was a suicide,
I was a soul overboard, and what I took
for a nipple was the nose of a shark.
But you! You walk the planks

each nanosecond casual as breathing,
you kiss like a shipwrecked Greek chorus
with seaweed for lungs— I mourn your mouth!
But meanwhile, there's Bach.

At least I remember how to sublimate.
With these Two-Part Inventions
I confirm the difference
between order and repetition— compulsion.

My left hand's a flying fish,
my right hand's a swimming bird—
the hands collide in the horizon, couple,
and soar to heaven, which is underground.

See how easy to be passionate yet calm,
to drown and float at once?
You don't even have to be original:
Bach, like sex or *Hamlet*,

survives our infinite idiosyncrasy.
While millions may presently be playing
Number Fourteen in B Flat,
I'm willing to bet the first baby

we'll never have that not one of them
is thinking about how the Inventions
are like when it first turns winter
and you can't drown the feeling

that it *has* been winter all Fall,
that soon it will be Spring;
not one is haunted by you squatting
in front of the broken TV

with your darling morbidity to whine,
"Death is the termination of all matter"—
ah, Bach! Ah, poor friend! Go ahead,
jump. Give it up. I dare you.

Kafka Poem

Dusk or dawn, maybe a bridge;
I can't tell through the mist.
The tarnished statues of saints,
shadows warped on cobblestone.
I could have been born here.
It doesn't matter, it's always
the same: the invisible knife
in my back, the glitter
that leads me like an eyedog.

There are maps of every city in my brain.
The X on each map aches like a halo
around the stump
of a missing limb.
I look for change in phonebooths,
in puddles under streetlamps;
listen for hollow tiles
in the pews of churches.
Watch my hand disappear in the fog.

Someone is leaning over a bridge,
throwing scraps of paper in the river.
He says he wishes he could cry.
I smooth his hair, kiss the dark
eyes. There are doors gently
opening somewhere, there is sunrise
through them. Through one door
I can smell the lush green of a distant island:
we are drinking from a spring.

Father Animus and Zimmer

Father Animus asked who broke
The window in the sacristy.
I went head-on into evil,
Lying through my new incisors.

Holy Ghost moaned in my guts.
The light bulbs swayed on
Their chords in the parish
As each freckle on my face
Became a venial sin.

Father Animus asked his question,
My answer tangled in memories
Of ardor in the cozy parish:

How springtime I would swing up
Into dogwood trees in the churchyard,
Let the dark eyes of the blossoms read
Me like a breviary.
      Summertime
I ran the baselines as though
They were the shadow of the spire.

In fall, exploring the attic
Of the old grade school,
I became my own history in
The dust, finding my father's
Initials carved in a broken desk,

My aunts' and uncles' first communions
Crumbling in antique records.

One winter, when the janitor
Had sprained his ankle, I climbed
Up inside the steeple to free
The bell rope, rung after rung,
Through drafts and timberings.
Bats retreated, wind screeched
Outside through the slate shingles.
I felt I was rising in the head
Of Father Animus, through warnings
And pronouncements, his strict,
Reluctant love diminishing as
I aspired, choked, deprived
Of space as I climbed higher.

Father Animus asked who
Broke the sacristy window
And the cross on the spire,
Tucking in its legs,
Flew away in sorrow.

The Failings

1. The Philosophy of Ears

The other night the moon, which had grown hungry
And sad as the month wore on, bloomed and shown
In full within a broad ring above the valley.
I understand that many sounds attended this event:
The huge, collective pumping of peepers in wet grass,
Dog howls, and crickets sawing ardently on darkness,
But this vision of the moon came to me in silence.

And so it is time to develop the philosophy of ears.
Simple as this, if the kinglet sitting unseen on a sunlit

Branch raises its sweet, diminutive head to chatter
And I do not hear it, that kinglet does not exist.
If a flock of crows comes yacking and fouling through
Our fields, drilling its uproar through my hearing aids
Into the center of my head, then these crows exist.

2. Detachment

One spring morning I awoke imagining
All my visionary options still were open,
But then, swirling inside my left
Eyeball, came a black blizzard.

Detached retina, the doctor told me,
Reducing all my options to but three:
A slow withdrawal into darkness,
A buckle stitched around my eyeball,
Or a bubble inserted into my humor.
One unacceptable, two frightening,
I chose the third to gently nudge
My retina back into its place.

Now, despite its healing,
The drab inconstancy of
My left eye becomes apparent.
It has declared its difference,
Denies kinship with the right,
Goes the way of dullness and self-pity.
I swear by the fresh gods of spring
That I will not follow its example.

3. Skin

Beginning as a perfect zero
Skin was inescapable memory.
It started sketching on itself
When at first it felt
The pain of air,

Making lists, assuming
The light of sun
Or moon into its layers.

At length it abandoned purity,
Believed only in constant change,
Doubling and quadrupling to
Become a kind of semaphore:
Red for health, green for sickness,
Descending grey for anger,
A roily pink for love.

Tainted by rage, burned by lust,
And dried to papyrus by boredom,
It spent decades shedding
And repairing itself.
Now, anguished by its imperfection
And futility of its duties,
It moves again to flawless zero.

The Queen

The first time I saw her, light was falling,
Air was rich like the last days of autumn.
Despite her dazzle and warmth I was melancholy,
As I have always been in the presence of great power.

From then on I tried every day to be decent.
When I was crass, her lovely shoulders
Drooped like finished tulips in the garden.

I did not want to wait, and yet I waited
As I had never done before, and surely
In time the delicate snows began to fall.

So the glory of my restraint inspired me.
I became eloquent, attentive, civilized.
Times I had to say goodbye to her became
the greatest burdens of my onerous life.

Although there had never been any doubt,
I was constantly afraid. I thought perhaps
A god might come and take her from me.

Somehow it pleased me that others admired her,
Yet it made my knuckles
Turn white like worried children.

Contributors Notes

Ellery Akers lives in San Francisco. Her first book, *Knocking on the Earth*, was published by Wesleyan University Press in 1989. She is working on a book of nature essays, *Alive With the Others*.

Diane Averill lives in Portland, Oregon. Her first book, *Branches Doubled Over With Fruit*, was published by the University of Central Florida Press in 1991. She has taught at Lewis & Clark College and Portland Community College.

Marvin Bell is a poet, essayist and teacher. His most recent book of poetry is *Iris of Creation*. Brought up on eastern Long Island, New York, Mr. Bell lives in Iowa City, Iowa, where since 1965 he has been on the faculty of the Writers' Workshop, and in Port Townsend, Washington.

James Bertolino has received a Book-of-the-Month Club Poetry Fellowship, a Discovery Award and an NEA Fellowship. Carnegie Mellon University Press published his *New & Selected Poems* in 1978, and in 1986 *First Credo* was issued from the *Quarterly Review of Literature* Poetry Series. He lives on Guemes Island, north of Seattle, Washington.

Michael Blumenthal is Senior Lecturer in English at Harvard. His first book, *Sympathetic Magic*, was winner of the 1980 Watermark Poets of North America First Book Award. His other books include *Days We Would Rather Know* (Viking, 1984), *Laps* (University of Massachusetts, 1984), and *The Wages of Goodness* (Missouri, 1992).

Anne C. Bromley's first collection of poems, *Midwinter Transport*, was published by Carnegie Mellon in 1985. She is also the co-translator (from the Spanish and the Galician) of *Poems by Rosalia de Castro*, which was published by State University of New York Press in 1991.

T. Alan Broughton has published five novels, a collection of stories, and five books of poems. His most recent volume of poetry is *In the Country of Elegies*. He is the recipient of fellowships from the Guggenheim Foundation and the NEA. Broughton teaches at the University of Vermont.

Michael Dennis Browne's books include *The Sun Fetcher, Smoke from the Fires*, and *You Won't Remember This*. He has written many texts for music. He teaches and directs the creative writing program at the University of Minnesota in Minneapolis.

Ann Carrel sent her poems to *Three Rivers Poetry Journal* back in 1980 when she was an undergraduate at Kansas State University.

Kelly Cherry, novelist and poet, teaches at the University of Wisconsin. Her recent books are *My Life & Dr. Joyce Brothers* (Algonquin) and *Natural Theology* (Louisiana State University Press).

Gillian Conoley is the author of *Tall Stranger* (Carnegie Mellon, 1991), a nominee for the National Book Critics' Circle Award. Her other books include *Some Gangster Pain* (Carnegie Mellon, 1987), and *Woman Speaking Inside Film Noir* (Lynx House Press,

1984). Born in Taylor, Texas, Conoley now lives in San Francisco, where she teaches at Santa Clara University.

Peter Cooley was born in Detroit, Michigan. Since 1975 he has lived in New Orleans, where he is a professor of English at Tulane University. His books of poetry include *The Company of Strangers* (Missouri, 1975), and *The Room Where Summer Ends, Nightseasons, The Van Gogh Notebook,* and *The Astonished Hours,* all from Carnegie Mellon.

Michael Cuddihy was born in New York City the year FDR was first elected. He attended Notre Dame for two years before being sidelined for a time with polio. His works include a translation of Jacques Maritain's *The Peasant of the Garonne* (Holt, Rinehart, 1956); a chapbook of poetry, *Celebrations* (Copper Canyon, 1988); and book of poems, *A Walled Garden* (Carnegie Mellon, 1989). Founder of the defunct *Ironwood,* he currently lives in Tucson, Arizona.

Philip Dacey, born in St. Louis in 1939, is the author of five books of poetry and the co-editor of *Strong Measures: Contemporary American Poetry in Traditional Forms.* His honors include NEA, Pushcart and Fulbright awards. In 1990, he resigned from full-time teaching at Southwest State University in Marshall, Minnesota, in order to write poetry.

Carl Dennis teaches in the English Department at SUNY-Buffalo. His most recent book of poems, *Meetings with Time,* was published by Viking/Penguin.

Gregory Djanikian was born in Alexandria, Egypt, in 1949 and came to the United States in 1957. He is the author of two collections of poetry, *The Man in the Middle* and *Falling Deeply into America.* He is a lecturer in the writing program at the University of Pennsylvania.

Patricia Dobler lives in Pittsburgh, Pennsylvania, and directs the creative writing program at Carlow College. She is a Brittingham Prize winner and author of the recent *UXB* from Mill Hunk Books.

Stephen Dobyns has published 13 novels and seven books of poetry. His most recent novel is *After Shocks/Near Escapes* (Viking, 1991), and his most recent book of poems is *Body Traffic* (Viking, 1991). He is director of the creative writing program at Syracuse University.

Wayne Dodd has been for many years director of the creative writing program at Ohio University. He is the author of *Echoes of the Unspoken,* published by University of Georgia Press.

Rita Dove's third book of poetry, *Thomas and Beulah,* received the 1987 Pulitzer Prize. Her most recent publications include *Grace Notes* (poetry, 1989) and *Through the Ivory Gate* (novel, 1992). A professor of English at the University of Virginia, Ms. Dove lives in Charlottesville with her husband, the novelist Fred Viebahn, and their daughter, Aviva.

Stephen Dunn is the author of eight collections of poetry, four of which were published by Carnegie Mellon. His work has won many awards, including the Levinson and Oscar Blumenthal Prizes from *Poetry,* and the Theodore Roethke Prize from *Poetry Northwest.* He is a Trustee Fellow in the Arts at Stockton State College in New Jersey.

Cornelius Eady lives in New York City. He is the author of *Victims of the Latest Dance Craze*, which won the 1985 Lamont Award. His most recent book, *The Gathering of My Name*, was published by Carnegie Mellon in 1991. Eady teaches at SUNY-Stony Brook where he directs the The Poetry Center.

Lynn Emanuel is an associate professor of English at the University of Pittsburgh. She is the author of *Hotel Fiesta* (University of Georgia Press) and *The Dig*, which was selected by Gerald Stern for the National Poetry Series and published by the University of Illinois Press. She was born in 1949 in New York City.

Ruth Fainlight's collections of poems include *Cages*, *To See the Matter Clearly*, *Another Full Moon*, *Sibyls and Others*, and *Fifteen to Infinity*, which was published by Carnegie Mellon in 1986. She lives in London with her husband, the writer Alan Sillitoe.

Charles Fort is an associate professor of English at Southern Connecticut State University in New Haven. He founded and for eight years directed the creative writing program at the University of North Carolina at Wilmington. Carnegie Mellon reissued his first collection, *The Town Clock Burning* (St. Andrews Press, 1985), under its Classic Contemporaries series in 1991.

Brendan Galvin lives in the woods above a Cape Cod marsh, and has taught college literature and writing courses for more than 20 years. His most recent books are *The Saints in their Oxhide Boat* (LSU) and *Early Returns* (Carnegie Mellon).

Gary Gildner's published work includes *Blue Like the Heavens* (new and selected poems), *The Second Bridge* (a novel), *A Week in South Dakota* (short stories), and *The Warsaw Sparks* (a memoir). He has received the National Magazine Award for Fiction, a number of poetry prizes, and two fellowships from the NEA. During 1988 he was Fulbright Lecturer at the University of Warsaw and coach of the city's baseball team.

Patricia Goedicke teaches in the department of English at the University of Montana. Milkweed Editions published her most recent book, *The Tongues We Speak: New & Selected Poems*, in 1989.

Jim Hall teaches at Florida International University in Miami. Known for his poems to readers of *Three Rivers Poetry Journal* and of the Carnegie Mellon Poetry Series, he has of late embarked on a new career as a writer of thrillers, which include *Under Cover of Daylight* and *Bones of Coral*.

C. G. Hanzlicek is director of the creative writing program at California State University at Fresno, where he has been teaching since 1966. His books of poetry are *Living in It*, *Stars*, *Calling the Dead*, *A Dozen for Leah*, and *When There Are No Secrets*. He has also published two volumes of translations.

James Harms was born in 1960 in Pasadena, California. He holds a degree in English from the University of Redlands and an M.F.A. from Indiana University. His first book, *Modern Ocean*, was published by Carnegie Mellon in 1992. He has taught at the University of Redlands, Denison University, and East Stroudsburg University.

Richard Harteis' books of poetry include *Fourteen Women*, *Morocco Journal* and *Internal Geography*, each published by Carnegie Mellon. He edited an anthology of Bulgarian poetry, *Window on the Black Sea* (Carnegie Mellon, 1992), and his non-fiction book, *Marathon*, was published by W. W. Norton in 1989. He lives in Bethesda, Maryland.

Brooks Haxton, originally from Mississippi, is the author of four books including the hilarious *The Lay of Eleanor and Irene, Dead Reckoning*, and *Traveling Company*.

Ann Hayes has taught for many years in the English department of Carnegie Mellon University. Her book, *The Living and the Dead*, was the first title in the Carnegie Mellon Poetry Series. She lives in Pittsburgh.

Judy Page Heitzman lives in Marshfield, Massachusetts. Her work has appeared in *The New Yorker* and several literary magazines.

Jonathan Holden is a University Distinguished Professor (English) and Poet-in-Residence at Kansas State University. His most recent books are *The Fate of American Poetry* and *American Gothic* (poems), both from the University of Georgia Press. Holden has won numerous awards for his poetry, including the 1985 Juniper Prize, the 1983 AWP award, and the 1972 Devins Award.

Colette Inez, author of five books of poetry, received fellowships from the Guggenheim and Rockefeller Foundations, and twice from the NEA. Widely published, she has taught at Ohio and Bucknell universities, Kalamazoo College, The New School, and is currently on the faculty of Columbia University's writing program.

David James received his B.A. from Western Michigan University and his M.A. from Central Michigan University. His book, *A Heart Out of This World*, was published by Carnegie Mellon in 1984. He is married, has three children, and works as director of admissions for the University of Michigan at Flint.

Mark Jarman is the author of four collections of poetry, *North Sea, The Rote Walker, Far and Away*, and *The Black Riviera*, and a book-length poem, *Iris*. He is the recipient of a Joseph Henry Jackson Award, two grants from the NEA, and a Guggenheim Fellowship. His *The Black Riviera* was co-winner of the 1991 Poets' Prize. He teaches at Vanderbilt.

David Keller grew up in a small Iowa town. His poems claim he was educated in the theaters and orchestra pits of the Boston area, though he attended several colleges. His first book, *A New Room*, was published in the QRL Poetry Series in 1987, and *Land That Wasn't Ours* appeared in 1989 (Carnegie Mellon). He also performs with the stilt-walking troupe called, Clark Kent.

Mary Kinzie teaches at Northwestern University where she is director of the creative writing program. She is the author of four collections of poems, including the recent *Autumn Eros and Other Poems* (Knopf).

Elizabeth Kirschner's first book of poems, *Twenty Colors*, was published by Carnegie Mellon in 1992. Her poems have appeared in *The Ohio Review, The Gettysburg Review, The Georgia Review* and elsewhere. She lives in Chestnut Hill, Massachusetts, and teaches at Boston College.

Ted Kooser makes his living as an insurance executive in Lincoln, Nebraska. A longtime contributor to *Three Rivers Poetry Journal*, his *Sure Signs: New & Selected Poems* was published by the University of Pittsburgh Press.

Larry Levis recently has moved to Richmond, Virginia. He is the author of five collections of poetry, including *The Dollmaker's Ghost, Winter Stars*, and *The Widening Spell of the Leaves*. He is the recipient of numerous awards, among them a Guggenheim Fellowship in 1983, three fellowships from the NEA, the Lamont Prize for Poetry in 1976, and a Fulbright Fellowship to Yugoslavia.

Elizabeth Libbey lives with her husband, the writer William H. MacLeish, in western Massachusetts. She teaches at Trinity College in Hartford and has published three books of poems, *The Crowd Inside, Songs of a Returning Soul*, and *All That Heat in a Cold Sky*, all from Carnegie Mellon.

Thomas Lux has published many chapbooks and five full-length collections, the latest of which are, respectively, *A Boat In The Forest* (Adastra, 1992) and *The Drowned River* (Houghton Mifflin, 1990). He teaches at Sarah Lawrence College.

Jack Matthews lives in Athens, Ohio, where he is Distinguished Professor of English at Ohio University. In addition to his collection of poems, he has published novels and books of short stories and non-fiction. He is a renowned bibliophile, and has often written about the world of old and rare books.

Mekeel McBride is an associate professor of English at the University of New Hampshire. She has also taught at Harvard, Princeton and Wheaton. Grants include a Bunting Institute Fellowship and two NEAs. Ms. McBride has three books with Carnegie Mellon: *No Ordinary World* (1979), *The Going Under of the Evening Land* (1983), and *Red Letter Days* (1988).

Heather McHugh's books include *Shades*, published by Wesleyan University Press.

Wesley McNair is the author of *The Faces of Americans in 1853* (Missouri) and *The Town of No* (Godine). He lives on Chicken Street in Mercer, Maine.

Jay Meek has published five books in the Carnegie Mellon Poetry Series, including *Windows* (1994). He has received grants from the NEA, the Guggenheim Foundation, and the Bush Foundation. Currently, he directs the writing program at the University of North Dakota, where he is poetry editor of *North Dakota Quarterly*.

William Meissner lives in St. Cloud, Minnesota. His collections of poems are *Learning to Breathe Underwater* and *The Sleepwalker's Son*, both from Ohio University Press.

Leslie Adrienne Miller's second collection of poems, *Ungodliness*, is forthcoming from Carnegie Mellon in 1994. She is also the author of *Staying Up for Love* (1990) and *No River*, winner of the Stanley Hanks Memorial Award from St. Louis Poetry Center in 1987. She is currently an assistant professor of poetry at the University of St. Thomas in St. Paul, Minnesota.

Linda Mizejewski received her Ph.D. in film studies from the University of Pittsburgh.

Veronica Morgan has had poems in *Three Rivers Poetry Journal* on two occasions. She lives in Amherst, Massachusetts.

Ed Ochester has published nine collections of poetry, most recently *Changing the Name to Ochester* (1988) and *Miracle Mile* (1984), each from Carnegie Mellon. He is director of the writing program at the University of Pittsburgh, editor of the Pitt Poetry Series and, for 1991-92, president of Associated Writing Programs.

Mary Oliver's *New and Selected Poems* appeared from Beacon Press in 1992. Among her many awards are the Pulitzer Prize for Poetry and the Shelley Memorial Award. She has lived for many years in Provincetown, Massachusetts, and recently served as Writer-in-Residence at Sweet Briar College in Virginia.

Rosalind Pace has published poems in *Three Rivers Poetry Journal* as well as *Denver Quarterly*, *Ontario Review*, and other magazines. She lives on Cape Cod.

Linda Pastan lives in Potomac, Maryland. She has published eight volumes of poetry, including *The Imperfect Paradise* (1988) and *Heroes in Disguise* (1991), both from Norton.

Ricardo Pau-Llosa, a native of Havana, has lived in Florida since 1960. He is an art critic specializing in modern Latin American art, and a curator. Pau-Llosa's poetry titles are *Sorting Metaphors* (Anhinga Prize, 1983), *Bread of the Imagined* (Bilingual Press, Arizona State University, 1991), and *Cuba* (Carnegie Mellon, 1993). He is currently an associate professor of English in Miami-Dade Community College, South Campus.

Anne S. Perlman, a former journalist in Paris and San Francisco, has led poetry workshops at the Squaw Valley Community of Writers and San Francisco's Washington High School. Her first collection of poems, *Sorting it Out*, was published by Carnegie Mellon in 1982.

Joyce Peseroff was born in New York City in 1948. Her books include, *A Dog in the Lifeboat* (Carnegie Mellon), *The Hardness Scale, Robert Bly: When Sleepers Awake*, and *The Ploughshares Poetry Reader*. She has received grants from the Massachusetts Artists Foundation and the NEA. Currently she teaches writing and literature at Emerson College in Boston.

Adora Phillips was a creative writing major at Carnegie Mellon University. After working in publishing in New York City, she lived briefly in Seattle and now lives abroad.

Carol J. Pierman has published two books of poetry, *The Naturalized Citizen* (New Rivers Press) and *The Age of Krypton* (Carnegie Mellon). Her work has appeared recently in *Iowa Review*, *Carolina Quarterly*, and *Black Warrior Review*. She teaches at the University of Alabama.

Lawrence Raab is the author of three collections of poems: *Other Children*, *The Collector of Cold Weather*, and *Mysteries of the Horizon*. He has received the Bess Hokin Prize from *Poetry*, a Junior Fellowship from the University of Michigan Society of Fellows, and grants from the NEA and the Massachusetts Council on the Arts. He teaches writing and literature at Williams College.

Thomas Rabbitt, who lives and works on a horse farm in Elrod, Alabama, has been employed by the University of Alabama since 1972. His first book, *Exile*, won the United States Award and was published in 1974. His work has appeared in numerous publications, including *Poetry*, *Black Warrior Review*, and *Shenandoah*.

Paula Rankin is an associate professor of English at Hampton University and lives in Newport News, Virginia. She is the author of four poetry collections: *By the Wreckmaster's Cottage*, *Augers*, *To the House Ghost*, and *Divorce: A Romance*, all published by Carnegie Mellon.

Rush Rankin has published in *Three Rivers Poetry Journal* several times over the years. He teaches at the Kansas City Art Institute.

Donald Revell is the author of several books including *New Dark Ages* and *The Gaza of Winter*. He teaches at the University of Denver.

Judith Root's first book, *Weaving the Sheets*, was reprinted by Carnegie Mellon after being published in a fine print edition by Abattoir. She is currently living in Idaho, teaching at Boise State University and completing a second collection. Her poems have appeared recently in *The Nation*, *American Poetry Review*, *Poetry*, and *The Paris Review Anthology*.

Trish Rucker sent her work for *Three Rivers Poetry Journal* from Stone Mountain, Georgia.

Vern Rutsala's books, in addition to those published by Carnegie Mellon, are *The Window*, *Laments*, *The Journey Begins*, *Paragraphs*, *Backtracking*, and *Selected Poems*. He has received fellowships from the Guggenheim Foundation and the NEA, as well as the Masters Fellowship from the Oregon Arts Commission. He teaches at Lewis and Clark College.

Jeannine Savard's first book, *Snow Water Cove*, won the University of Utah Press annual poetry competition for 1988. Her poems have appeared in *Antioch Review*, *Poetry Northwest*, and *North American Review*. She teaches at Arizona State University. Carnegie Mellon published her second book, *Trumpeter*, in 1993.

Laurie Schorr, formerly an undergraduate at Carnegie Mellon University, received her M.A. from Johns Hopkins, an M.F.A. from Arizona, and is currently a Ph.D. candidate at the University of Arizona. She now calls herself Laurie MacDiarmid.

Eve Shelnutt has published *Air and Salt* (1983), *Recital in a Private Home* (1989), and *First a Long Hesitation* (1992) with Carnegie Mellon. She has published short story collections, two books on the craft of writing, and has edited three anthologies of essays. She lives in Athens, Ohio.

Georgia Sine is a former student in the creative writing program at Carnegie Mellon University. She currently is living in Minneapolis, where she is a graduate student at the University of Minnesota.

John Skoyles' first book of poems, *A Little Faith*, was published in 1981. He has received grants from the New York State Foundation for the Arts, the North Carolina Arts Council, and two fellowships from the NEA. Until recently he directed the M.F.A. Program for Writers at Warren Wilson College. He now lives in Provincetown.

Dave Smith has published 10 books of poetry, including *The Fisherman's Whore* (recently reprinted by Carnegie Mellon), and two books of fiction. Among collections he has edited are *The Morrow Anthology of Younger American Poets* and *The Pure Clear Word: Essays On the Poetry of James Wright*. He lives in Baton Rouge.

Marcia Southwick has published two books of poems: *The Night Won't Save Anyone* (University of Georgia) and *Why the River Disappears* (Carnegie Mellon). She has been a Visiting Poet at the University of Iowa Writers' Workshop and the University of Colorado at Boulder. At present, she is an associate professor at the University of Nebraska at Lincoln.

Primus St. John lives in West Linn, Oregon. He has published three books: *Skins on the Earth* (Copper Canyon), and *Love is Not a Consolation; It Is a Light*, and *Dreamer* (both Carnegie Mellon).

Kim R. Stafford grew up in Oregon, Iowa, Indiana, California, and Alaska. He has published nine books of poetry and prose, including *Having Everything Right: Essays of Place* (Confluence Press, 1986). He directs the Northwest Writing Institute at Lewis & Clark College in Portland.

William Stafford's new collection from Confluence Press is *My Name is William Tell*. He continues to live in Portland.

Maura Stanton won the Yale Series of Younger Poets Award for her first book of poetry, *Snow On Snow* (Yale University Press, 1975). *Cries of Swimmers* was first published by the University of Utah Press in 1984, and reprinted in Carnegie Mellon's Classic Contemporaries series. *Tales of the Supernatural* was published by David R. Godine in 1988. She teaches in the M.F.A. program at Indiana University at Bloomington.

Gerald Stern has taught for a number of years in the creative writing program at the University of Iowa. His collections of poems include *Lucky Life*, *The Red Coal*, *Paradise Poems*, *Lovesick*, and *Leaving Another Kingdom: Selected Poems*. *Bread Without Sugar*, his tenth collection, has just been published by Norton.

James Tate, a native of Kansas City, Missouri, currently teaches at the University of Massachusetts at Amherst. His first book, *The Lost Pilot*, won the Yale Series of Younger Poets Award. He has published many books, including *The Oblivion Ha-Ha* (1970), *Hints to Pilgrims* (1971), *Viper Jazz* (1976), *Constant Defender* (1983), and *Distance from Loved Ones* (1990). His *Selected Poems* was published in the spring of 1991, and subsequently awarded the Pulitzer Prize for Poetry.

Alberta Turner was for many years director of the Poetry Center at Cleveland State University. The author of *A Belfry of Knees* and *Responses to Poetry*, she lives in Oberlin, Ohio.

Lee Upton is from Michigan. Currently, she teaches at Lafayette College in Pennsylvania. Her most recent book, *No Mercy*, was selected by James Tate for the National Poetry Series.

Robert Wallace was born in Missouri in 1932 and has lived since 1965 in Cleveland, Ohio, where he teaches at Case Western Reserve University. His most recent publications are *The Common Summer: New and Selected Poems* (1989) and the textbook, *Writing Poems* (3rd edition, 1991).

Michael Waters teaches at Salisbury State University on the eastern shore of Maryland. He has also taught at Ohio University, and has served as Visiting Professor of American Literature at the University of Athens, Greece, and as Banister Writer-in-Residence at Sweet Briar College. He has published five volumes of poetry, including *Anniversary of the Air* (1985), *The Burden Lifters* (1989), and *Bountiful* (1992) from Carnegie Mellon.

Dara Wier's books include *Blood, Hook & Eye* (1977), *The 8-Step Grapevine* (1980), *All You Have in Common* (1984), *The Book of Knowledge* (1988), and *Blue for the Plough* (1992). A recipient of fellowships from the Guggenheim Foundation and the NEA, she teaches at the University of Massachusetts at Amherst. She was born in New Orleans.

Renate Wood was born in Berlin and educated in Europe before earning degrees from Stanford and Warren Wilson. *Raised Underground* (Carnegie Mellon, 1991) is her first book-length collection of poetry. She teaches at the University of Colorado at Boulder and the Warren Wilson M.F.A. Program for Writers.

C. D. Wright's sixth collection of poetry, *String Light*, was published in 1991 by the University of Georgia Press. In 1992, *Just Whistle*, a book-length valentine with photographs by Deborah Luster, will be released by Kelsey Street Press (Berkeley). She is co-editor of Lost Roads Publishers, a book press, and teaches at Brown University.

Franz Wright was born in Vienna. He attended Oberlin College and spent his 20s traveling and writing. He has published six books of translation from French and German poets and 11 volumes of poetry, including *The Night World & the Word Night* (Carnegie Mellon, 1993). He lives in Everett, Massachusetts.

Karen Zealand published a chapbook of poems, *Wedding the Lovers Within*, in *Three Rivers Poetry Journal* (33/34). She lives in LaVale, Maryland.

Lisa Zeidner, a former undergraduate student at Carnegie Mellon University, received advanced degrees from Johns Hopkins and Washington University. She is the author of three novels. Her most recent book of poems is *Pocket Sundial* (Wisconsin, 1988).

Paul Zimmer is director of the University of Iowa Press. He is the author of many volumes of poetry, including *Family Reunion* (University of Pittsburgh Press) and *The Great Bird of Love* (Illinois), which was chosen by William Stafford for the National Poetry Series.

About the Editors

Gerald Costanzo's books include *In the Aviary* (University of Missouri Press), *The Laps of the Bridesmaids* (Bits Press), and *Nobody Lives on Arthur Godfrey Boulevard* (BOA Editions). He began teaching at Carnegie Mellon University in 1970 and founded the University Press in 1975.

Jim Daniels is the author of three books of poetry, *Places/Everyone* (University of Wisconsin Press), *Punching Out* (Wayne State University Press), and *M-80* (University of Pittsburgh Press). He is an associate professor at Carnegie Mellon.

Kathleen Samudovsky is a Pittsburgh area free-lance writer working on graduate degrees in journalism and professional writing. A former newspaper reporter, she studied poetry at Carnegie Mellon in the late 1980s.

First Publication Credits

Poems published in Carnegie Mellon books originally appeared in the following publications. Those not listed here first appeared in *Three Rivers Poetry Journal*.

Marvin Bell: "Stars Which See, Stars Which Do Not See" and "The Mystery of Emily Dickinson," *The New Yorker*; "Gemwood," *Field*.

James Bertolino: "The Coons," *The New Salt Creek Reader*; "On a Line by John Ashbery," *Bonewhistle*; "The Landscape," *The Painted Bride Quarterly*.

Anne C. Bromley: "Slow Men Working in Trees," *Massachusetts Review*; "Teel St. Trailer Court," *Poet and Critic*.

T. Alan Broughton: "Lyric," *Poetry*; "Hold, Hold" and "Serenade for Winds," *Virginia Quarterly Review*.

Gillian Conoley: "Some Gangster Pain," *Ploughshares*; "I'd Like a Little Love in the Wine-red Afternoon," *College English*; "Unchained Melody," *Denver Quarterly*.

Peter Cooley: "Ararat," *The Georgia Review*; "The Elect," *The Ohio Review*; "The Other," *The New Yorker*.

Philip Dacey: "Small Dark Song," *Counter/Measures*; "Porno Love," *Massachusetts Review*; "Looking at Models in the Sears Catalogue," *Heartland II: Poets of the Midwest*.

Gregory Djanikian: "Agami Beach," *Iowa Review*; "When I First Saw Snow" and "How I Learned English," *Poetry*.

Stephen Dobyns: "Black Dog, Red Dog," *The American Poetry Review*; "What You Have Come to Expect," *The New Yorker*; "The Gun," *Antaeus*; "General Matthei Drives Home Through Santiago," *Poetry*.

Rita Dove: "Weathering Out," *Agni Review*; "The Event," *Ohio Review*; "Parsley," *Ontario Review*.

Charles Fort: "The Worker (We Own Two Houses)," *A New Geography of Poets*; "How Old Are the People of the World," *Portfolio*.

Gary Gildner: "Cabbage in Polish" and "String," *Poetry*; "Primarily We Miss Ourselves As Children," *River Styx*.

C. G. Hanzlicek: "Room for Doubt," *Quarterly West*.

James Harms: "Breakfast on the Patio," *The Southern Poetry Review*; "Explaining the Evening News to Corbyn," *The Kenyon Review*; "My Androgynous Years," *Crazyhorse*.

Richard Harteis: "The Hermit's Curse," *Seneca Review*; "Mirage," *Small Pond*.

Jonathan Holden: "Losers," *Poetry*; "Falling from Stardom," *Crazyhorse*; "Liberace," *Midwest Quarterly*.

Colette Inez: "The Woman Who Loved Worms," *Four Quarters*; "Slumnight," *Poetry Bag*; "Instructions for the Erection of a Statue to Myself in Central Park," *The Fiddlehead*.

David James: "Harvest," *Quarterly West*; "The Love of Water Faucets," *Centennial Review*.

Mark Jarman: "Cavafy in Redondo," *The New Yorker*; "The Mirror," *The Sonora Review*; "The Supremes," *The New Yorker*.

David Keller: "Mussels," *Ohio Review*.

Elizabeth Kirschner: "Two Blue Swans," *The North American Review*.

Larry Levis: "For Zbigniew Herbert, Summer, 1971, Los Angeles," *Field*.

Elizabeth Libbey: "Spring And," *The Atlantic*; "Come Into the Night Grove," *The New Yorker*; "Juana Bautista Lucero, Circa 1926, to Her Photographer," *Ascent*.

Thomas Lux: "Solo Native," *Antaeus*; "Gold on Mule" and "Barn Fire," *Ploughshares*.

Mekeel McBride: "Loneliness," *Tendril*; "The Going Under of the Evening Land," *Aspen Anthology*; "Red Letters," *Ontario Review*.

Jay Meek: "Vienna in the Rain," *The Kenyon Review*.

Leslie Adrienne Miller: "My Students Catch Me Dancing" and "The Weather of Invention," *Quarterly West*.

Ed Ochester: "The Relatives," *Poetry*; "The Canaries in Uncle Arthur's Basement," *Virginia Quarterly Review*; "New Day," *Poetry*.

Ricardo Pau-Llosa: "Ostiones Y Cangrejos Moros," *New England Review*; "Frutas," *Kenyon Review*; "Ganaderia," *Michigan Quarterly Review*.

Anne S. Perlman: "Summer Adjustments," *Hudson Review*; "Survival," *The Nation*; "Family Reunion," *The Paris Review*.

Joyce Peseroff: "Bluebird," *New Letters*; "Adolescent," *Harvard Magazine*; "A Dog in the Lifeboat," *Massachusetts Review*.

Carol J. Pierman: "Eight Cows," *Carolina Quarterly*.

Lawrence Raab: "The Room," *Poetry*; "The Witch's Story," *The New Yorker*; "For You," *Poetry*; "On the Island," *Quarterly West*.

Thomas Rabbitt: "My Father's Watch," *Ploughshares*; "Tortoise," *The Black Warrior Review*.

Judith Root: "Naming the Shells," *The Nation*; "Snail Winter," *The New Republic*.

Vern Rutsala: "Skaters," *Poetry*.

Jeannine Savard: "The Daughter's Brooch," *Ploughshares*; "The Fall," *The North American Review*; "A Carnival Figure of Guatemalan Clay," *The American Poetry Review*; "The Descent of Fire," *The Kenyon Review*.

Eve Shelnutt: "The Triumph of Children," *North American Review*; "O Hero," *Chattahoochee Review*.

John Skoyles: "Good Cheer," *TriQuarterly*.

Marcia Southwick: "The Ruins" and "The Sun Speaks," *The American Poetry Review*.

Maura Stanton: "Childhood," *Poetry*; "Shoplifters," *The Atlantic*.

James Tate: "Deaf Girl Playing," *Mediterranean Review*.

Robert Wallace: "The Double Play," *Poetry*; "In a Spring Still Not Written Of," *Harper's Magazine*.

Michael Waters: "Keats' Lips," *Ironwood*; "Miles Weeping," *The American Poetry Review*; "The Mystery of the Caves," *Poetry*.

Renate Wood: "Blood," *Prairie Schooner*; "The Pilot" and "Cabbages," *The American Poetry Review*.

C. D. Wright: "Scratch Music," *Five Fingers Review*; "This Couple," *The New Yorker*.

Franz Wright: "The Needle: For a Friend Who Disappeared," *The New Yorker*; "Joseph Come Back As the Dusk (1950-1982)" and "Pawtucket Postcards," *Field*; "Entry in an Unknown Hand," *Paris Review*.

Carnegie Mellon Poetry Series

1975
The Living and the Dead, Ann Hayes
In the Face of Descent, T. Alan Broughton

1976
The Week the Dirigible Came, Jay Meek
Full of Lust and Good Usage, Stephen Dunn

1977
How I Escaped from the Labyrinth and Other Poems, Philip Dacey
The Lady from the Dark Green Hills, Jim Hall
For Luck: Poems 1962-1977, H. L. Van Brunt
By the Wreckmaster's Cottage, Paula Rankin

1978
New & Selected Poems, James Bertolino
The Sun Fetcher, Michael Dennis Browne
A Circus of Needs, Stephen Dunn
The Crowd Inside, Elizabeth Libbey

1979
Paying Back the Sea, Philip Dow
Swimmer in the Rain, Robert Wallace
Far from Home, T. Alan Broughton
The Room Where Summer Ends, Peter Cooley
No Ordinary World, Mekeel McBride

1980
And the Man Who Was Traveling Never Got Home, H. L. Van Brunt
Drawing on the Walls, Jay Meek
The Yellow House on the Corner, Rita Dove
The 8-Step Grapevine, Dara Wier
The Mating Reflex, Jim Hall

1981
A Little Faith, John Skoyles
Augers, Paula Rankin
Walking Home from the Icehouse, Vern Rutsala
Work and Love, Stephen Dunn

The Rote Walker, Mark Jarman
Morocco Journal, Richard Harteis
Songs of a Returning Soul, Elizabeth Libbey

1982
The Granary, Kim R. Stafford
Calling the Dead, C. G. Hanzlicek
Dreams Before Sleep, T. Alan Broughton
Sorting It Out, Anne S. Perlman
Love Is Not a Consolation; It Is a Light, Primus St. John

1983
The Going Under of the Evening Land, Mekeel McBride
Museum, Rita Dove
Air and Salt, Eve Shelnutt
Nightseasons, Peter Cooley

1984
Falling from Stardom, Jonathan Holden
Miracle Mile, Ed Ochester
Girlfriends and Wives, Robert Wallace
Earthly Purposes, Jay Meek
Not Dancing, Stephen Dunn
The Man in the Middle, Gregory Djanikian
A Heart Out of This World, David James
All You Have in Common, Dara Wier

1985
Smoke from the Fires, Michael Dennis Browne
Full of Lust and Good Usage, Stephen Dunn (2nd edition)
Far and Away, Mark Jarman
Anniversary of the Air, Michael Waters
To the House Ghost, Paula Rankin
Midwinter Transport, Anne Bromley

1986
Seals in the Inner Harbor, Brendan Galvin
Thomas and Beulah, Rita Dove
Further Adventures With You, C. D. Wright
Fifteen to Infinity, Ruth Fainlight
False Statements, Jim Hall
When There Are No Secrets, C. G. Hanzlicek

1987
Some Gangster Pain, Gillian Conoley
Other Children, Lawrence Raab
Internal Geography, Richard Harteis
The Van Gogh Notebook, Peter Cooley
A Circus of Needs, Stephen Dunn (2nd edition)
Ruined Cities, Vern Rutsala
Places and Stories, Kim R. Stafford

1988
Preparing to Be Happy, T. Alan Broughton
Red Letter Days, Mekeel McBride
The Abandoned Country, Thomas Rabbitt
The Book of Knowledge, Dara Wier
Changing the Name to Ochester, Ed Ochester
Weaving the Sheets, Judith Root

1989
Recital in a Private Home, Eve Shelnutt
A Walled Garden, Michael Cuddihy
The Age of Krypton, Carol J. Pierman
Land That Wasn't Ours, David Keller
Stations, Jay Meek
The Common Summer: New and Selected Poems, Robert Wallace
The Burden Lifters, Michael Waters
Falling Deeply into America, Gregory Djanikian
Entry in an Unknown Hand, Franz Wright

1990
Why the River Disappears, Marcia Southwick
Staying Up For Love, Leslie Adrienne Miller
Dreamer, Primus St. John

1991
Permanent Change, John Skoyles
Clackamas, Gary Gildner
Tall Stranger, Gillian Conoley
The Gathering of My Name, Cornelius Eady
A Dog in the Lifeboat, Joyce Peseroff
Raised Underground, Renate Wood
Divorce: A Romance, Paula Rankin

1992
Modern Ocean, James Harms
The Astonished Hours, Peter Cooley
You Won't Remember This, Michael Dennis Browne
Twenty Colors, Elizabeth Kirschner
First A Long Hesitation, Eve Shelnutt
Bountiful, Michael Waters
Blue for the Plough, Dara Wier
All That Heat in a Cold Sky, Elizabeth Libbey

1993
Trumpeter, Jeannine Savard
Cuba, Ricardo Pau-Llosa

Carnegie Mellon Classic Contemporaries

Peter Balakian
Sad Days of Light

Marvin Bell
Stars Which See, Stars Which Do Not See

Stephen Dobyns
Black Dog, Red Dog

Rita Dove
The Yellow House on the Corner
Museum

Stephen Dunn
Full of Lust and Good Usage
Not Dancing

Charles Fort
The Town Clock Burning

Brendan Galvin
Early Returns

Colette Inez
The Woman Who Loved Worms

Denis Johnson
The Incognito Lounge

Greg Kuzma
Good News

Larry Levis
The Dollmaker's Ghost

Thomas Lux
Sunday

Jack Matthews
  An Almanac for Twilight

Dave Smith
  The Fisherman's Whore

Maura Stanton
  Cries of Swimmers
  Snow on Snow

Gerald Stern
  Two Long Poems

James Tate
  Absences